HITCHHIKING
IN AMERICA

Using the
Golden Thumb

Loralye
May the roads we travel
always bring us back together.
Dale

Published by Lies Told Press, Ltd.

Printed in The United States of America.

Carpenter, Dale.
  Hitchhiking in America: Using the Golden Thumb.

  Bibliography.
  Includes index.
  1. Hitchhiking - United States.
  2. Hitchhiking - Media.
  3. Hiking, Pedestrian tours - United States, General Works.
  4. United States - Travel.

GV199.4   1992   917.04 Car
ISBN 0-9631910-0-4

All illustrations by the author.

This book is dedicated to all of the people who passed me by while I was hitchhiking. May they someday realize what an interesting person they missed meeting.

My thanks go out to all of the hitchhikers that I have ever met and who offered friendship and advice. This book could have been written without them but it never would have been as good.

Thanks also go out to Daniel H. Garrison of Northwestern University who, by offering observations both as a fellow hitchhiker and as a fellow writer, measurably improved this book.

An unpayable debt is owed to my friends who, with their knowledge of my hopeless ability to spell and use proper punctuation, gently pointed out my errors.

Contents

I   Introduction 7

II   Hitchhiking: A Social Phenomena
in the History of America 9

III   Hitchhiking as Portrayed in the
Media: Newspapers, Magazines,
Books, Movies, Television 21

IV   Advice for the Hitchhiker:
1. Why Hitchhike 33
2. Planning Your Trip 39
3. Alone or With a Friend 42
4. What to Take Along 45
5. Women Hitchhikers 60

V   On the Road:
1. How to Thumb 69
2. Choosing the Spot 71
3. Tactics for Hitchhiking 77
4. You and the Driver 84
5. Road Hassles 91
6. Sleeping on the Road 95
7. Sex on the Road 101
8. Keeping a Journal 104
9. The All-Important Attitude 108

VI   Conclusions and Recommendations 111

VII   Bibliography 117

VIII   Movies Mentioning, Showing, or
About Hitchhiking 126

IX   Index 134

My grateful acknowledgements to these companies who provided permission to use the quotes in this book;

And/Or Press, Berkeley, California;
Associated Press, New York, New York;
Basic Books, Inc., New York, New York;
Bantam Doubleday Dell Publishing Group, Inc.,
    New York, New York;
The Boston Globe, Boston, Mass.;
Car and Driver, Ann Arbor, Michigan;
The Crown Publishing Group, New York, New York;
Harper's Magazine, New York, New York;
Little, Brown and Company, Boston, Mass.;
Macmillian Publishing Co., New York, New York;
William Morrow & Co., New York, New York;
The Nation Company, Inc., New York, New York;
The New Republic, Washington, D.C.;
The New York Times, New York, New York;
Newsday, Inc., Melville, New York;
Newsweek, New York, New York;
W.W. Norton & Company, Inc., New York, New York;
Penguin Books USA Inc., New York, New York;
Random House, Inc., New York, New York;
Saturday Evening Post, Indianapolis, Indiana;
Simon & Schuster, New York, New York;
University of Colorado at Denver, Center for Urban
    Transportation Studies, Denver, Colorado;
The Washington Post, Washington, D.C.

INTRODUCTION

I was in the car less than 3 minutes when the driver asked where I had started from. "Upstate New York", I said. "Where?", he asked. "Binghamton, New York. Just over the Pennsylvania border. I started at noon." "What?" he yelled. "You started at noon and you got down here by Washington already?" "Yes, I've been lucky getting rides." "Lucky, hell. You must have a Golden Thumb."

I do not consider myself to be in the same league as Devon Smith who claims to have hitchhiked 290,000 miles from 1947 to 1971 (1979 *Guinness Book of World Records*), or with Paul DiMaggio, the author of *The Hitchhiker's Field Manual,* or with the young lady who was crowned Miss Hitchhiker by the Mayor of the Bowery (*New York Times,* August 23, 1946). My present tally at the time of this writing is over 30,000 miles. I've hitchhiked while in high school, while in the service, while attending college, and while working. While most of my hitchhiking has been done in the eastern half of the nation, I have done several cross-country trips around the United States. I once hitchhiked from upstate New York to Los Angeles just to attend a friend's wedding.

I really started hitchhiking as a youngster. Living out in the country meant a walk into town if I wanted to go visit the library or go shopping for comics or to visit my friends. After walking for miles and miles in town, I and any of my brothers and sisters who went with me faced the walk back home. So it was with sore feet that we, hesitantly at first, turned around to oncoming cars and put out our thumbs. Mostly it was friends of the family that picked us up, mainly because they knew us and lived out that way as well. While in high school, if I stayed late for a sports practice or for some other afterschool activity, it was my thumb that helped me get home. Hitchhiking like this, in a familiar area where one knows many people, is the safest way to be introduced to the pleasures of traveling by thumb. Learning to hitchhike like this, it is only a matter of time until the thought occurs that one could easily

7

hitchhike to visit friends in another town, or to a concert somewhere, or off to see the world.

The main reason for writing this book is to help those individuals who are planning to hitchhike for any period of time, be it for one week or longer. It will also, I hope, improve the image of the hitchhiker by giving a general overview of how hitchhikers have been portrayed in newspapers, periodicals, books, television, and films, and how very often this image is false and misleading.

I can not teach you how to hitchhike. Like parenting, sex, driving a vehicle, sky diving, swimming, building a house, exercising, and many other activities, hitchhiking can only be learned by doing. But I believe that I can give you much useful information that will make it easier and less hazardous to learn.

Webster's Seventh New Collegiate Dictionary defines the verb "hitchhike": "to travel by securing free rides - to solicit or obtain (a free ride) - hitchhiker noun." The noun "hitchhiker" has often been used interchangeably and erroneously with the words "hobo", "tramp", and "bum". All of these words carry with them a sense that this person is an undesirable. Hitchhiking tends to be seen as an activity used mostly by the unemployed, runaways, and criminals. It needs to be looked at as a means of transportation and as an activity worthy in itself.

> "Let me here dispel a popular fallacy concerning this practice. A hitchhiker is not a bum, although a bum may be a hitchhiker! The difference is this. A bum is - a bum; trying to chisel the most out of people with the least amount of labor expended. A hitchhiker is a person who has a certain destination to reach, feels his imposition upon the general public, but is willing to earn his way, and often does, in any manner possible."
>
> "Thumb Fun"
> Samuel D. Zeidman,
> *Review of Reviews,* April 1937

HITCHHIKING IN AMERICA:
A SOCIAL PHENOMENON

"Always the road has determined whether wanderers be many or few, whether their travels shall be near or far, as well as the rate of their movements. Always it has offered prodigal sons an avenue of escape from their burdens. The more numerous and the better the roads, the more tempting the invitation to fly from unpleasant things of life."

"As a successful vagabonding adventure, it will only suit travelers who are young enough in spirit to try it; tough and resourceful enough to cope with its problems; and tolerant enough to forgive those people who make it difficult."

Hitchhiking is thoroughly ingrained in the history of America. As travelers moved west across America, first to explore, then to settle, other travelers moved with them, begging rides in any manner they could. They offered to pay for their ride by doing work in return, or by exchanging news from the places they had been and heard of, or by telling stories and tales of this wide and wonderful country. Some moved in hopes of improving their standing in life, others because they had run afoul of the law or of public opinion, others simply because they had the "wanderlust". In *Holiday* magazine of December 1955, there is an article about one such man, Daniel Pratt.

"For there is evidence that he roamed America for fifty years, from the backwoods of Maine to the newly broken sod of Kansas and the Dakotas. His name became a byword, like Johnny Appleseed."

"For twelve years he disappeared from Prattville. (Prattville, district of Chelsea, Massachusetts where he was born in 1809). In an era before there were railroads or even roads for the transportation of hoboes, he turned toward the growing West. He hitched rides with pioneer families, he rode Conestoga wagons rumbling across the Alleghenies to deliver goods to log-cabin stores."

"The frontier then was Illinois: Daniel Pratt ventured beyond, to Kansas and the Dakotas, always in search of new sights -- and some stranger's hospitality. As he traveled back and forth across the country, managing to live without effort, the notion of work became more and more alien to him. Graciously accepting a night's lodging and a free meal, he made his hosts feel that his presence honored their farmhouse, cabin, or wigwam."

"When he returned to Prattville, there was a strange look in his eyes. From the time he reappeared in Prattville, Daniel never had a permanent home. He lived only to travel -- and to talk. He had seen much on his journeys and what he had not seen, he could imagine. He recounted his adventures gustily, mixing fact and fiction and his own off-beat philosophy into a heady brew of original prose."

"Today but one worthy memorial remains of Daniel Pratt, who once was a living legend to thousands. The Dictionary of American Biography lists hundreds of illustrious Americans; after each name the occupation is given: banker, statesman, lawyer, scientist. The entry for the Great American Traveler, however, is the only one of its kind. It reads, plainly and proudly:
        "Daniel Pratt -- Vagrant" "

        Raphael David Blau,
        Holiday, December 1955

Other travelers in the American scene have been given praise for their depictions of travel in America. Jim Tully was a hobo who wrote about the hobo's life and troubles during the 1920's and 1930's. Jack London, John Steinbeck, and Woody Guthrie wrote and sang proudly and truthfully about such people's experiences. These writers, and others, wrote mainly about traveling by train, as the automobile and highway system had not come into wide enough usage to permit efficient hitchhiking by automobile. After the First World War, enough automobiles were in use to permit travelers to try to hitchhike toward their destinations. Articles started to appear in the media during the 1920's and 1930's about hitchhikers and their travels. The word "hitch hiker" first appeared in the *New York Times*

Index in 1926 and in the *Reader's Guide to Periodical Literature* in 1928.

> "Any experienced hiker can travel three hundred miles a day in the west or two hundred and fifty miles a day in the East, if he stays on the main highways and avoids walking through the suburbs or the big cities. That is rather better time than is made by the average automobile tourist, but the hiker is not wearied by continuous driving and does not have to wait for repairs to tires or engine. If he grows tired of riding he can always get out and walk for a few miles, and if the driver is slow or has engine trouble, he can leave him at the next crossroads and wait for a faster machine."
>
> "The last time I traveled in this manner from coast to coast, it took twelve and a half days to cover a route of nearly four thousand miles."
>
> "The trip cost just $17.63, mostly for food, though the unnecessary extravagance of a phone call from Chicago to New York is included in that modest budget."
>
> "The Art of Hitch-Hiking"
> Hugh Hardyman, *The New Republic,* July 29, 1931

During the period between the two World Wars, hitchhiking, if not considered socially respectable, was at least accepted. James Michener, in his wonderful memoir, *The World is My Home,* writes of many happy times spent hitchhiking during the 1920's and 1930's. He states that this was the period when cars became affordable for the average family and when they drove them, were glad to share them and show them off. When the Depression put many individuals out of work and home, they traveled by any means, looking for work. Since the majority of citizens were undergoing hardships of some manner, helping others who were in the same condition seemed the natural and correct course of action.

> "The steady growth of legislation against hitch-hikers seems to have been a result of returning prosperity and with it a more rigid enforcement of previously enacted bans. The hitch-hiker's heyday undoubtedly was during the depth of the Depression, when few coins jingled in any pocket and when there was a universal feeling that there must be a job in the next town."
>
> "For the most part the hitch-hiker was not regarded as a tramp. He was a transient, a victim of misfortune on his way to new and greener fields."
>
> "Business improvement, however, has thinned the ranks; and that in

itself may be testimony to the hitch-hiker's essentially good character --
he really wanted a job, and now he has found one."

New York Times, July 25, 1937
Copyright 1927 by The New York Times Company.
Reprinted by permission.

During World War II, gasoline rationing was in effect and it was
considered a part of the war effort to pick up hitchhikers, especially
if they were servicemen. The New York state government voted to
allow military servicemen in uniform to hitchhike in May of 1942.
Mrs. Franklin D. Roosevelt, our First Lady, gave a lift to a student
hitchhiker in 1935, according to *The New York Times* of Sept. 13,
1935. Even Emily Post, the arbiter of social manners, gave advice to
women workers who had to hitchhike to and from their place of
employment (*New York Times,* Dec. 23, 1942). The *New York Times*
on August 28, 1944 carried an article stating that the Colorado
Republican candidates for state and national offices planned to
campaign that fall by taking trains to the farthest areas of Colorado
and hitchhiking back to the capital.

This feeling of goodwill toward fellow travelers lasted after the
war ended and into the 1950's. Many motorists considered the
hitchhiker a welcome traveling companion. After the Second World
War, the Eisenhower administration greatly expanded the highway
system in this country with the start of the 43,000+ mile federal
Interstate Highway System. This greatly improved interstate
commerce by allowing the easy movement of raw materials and
goods from one marketplace to another, as well as improving the
national defense by allowing the rapid movement of troops and
supplies, if needed. With an improved highway system and defense
factories now producing automobiles instead of war materials, there
was a vast increase in travelers on the roads. But with the rise in the
number of people traveling by automobile in the United States, there
was a corresponding rise in highway crime. Many states banned
hitchhiking on the major highways in their states, or banned it
altogether. The hitchhiker came to be viewed as an undesirable part
of society, a possible robber, mugger, or worse.

Then came the 1960's and 1970's, the years of experimentation with lifestyles, the years of travel for many young people who yearned to see another part and stratum of life other the one they had grown up in. Hitchhiking was perfect for them because most did not have or could afford an automobile. Hitchhiking required very little money, was unstructured, was forever changing and fluid, and could lead you where you wanted to go, or take you where you were willing to go. Thousands walked onto the shoulders of roads in this nation and traveled. They were led on by dreams of the American travelers and adventurers, Lewis and Clark, Daniel Boone and Davy Crockett, Huck Finn and Tom Sawyer, Dean Moriarty and Jack Kerouac, and all the others they had read, seen, heard or dreamed of. A study published in 1985 in *Adolescence* magazine claimed to have investigated the personalities of 104 cross-country hitchhikers and found them to be independent, impulsive, having a high degree of tolerance to complexity and change, and a strong interest in interpersonal relationships. This bears out my own experiences with hitchhikers.

All throughout our history, hitchhiking has been an accepted part of life for anyone in the service. The military itself frowns upon it and says that it is illegal to hitchhike while in uniform, but I never heard of any serviceman getting more then a stern talking to for having done it. I was picked up by sergeants and officers many times while in uniform and asked if I knew that I was breaking the law. But after saying that yes, I did know that and was visiting my fiance, all I ever received was a "don't do it again" lecture. In 1942, New York State made it legal for military service men in uniform to hitchhike. I wonder if that law is still on the books. Most military enlisted men and women do not own a vehicle and find hitchhiking an easy way to travel on or around the base where they are stationed as well as a good way to travel back to where they are from. Enlisted personnel have an advantage over civilians when they are hitchhiking in uniform. This is because civilians know about servicemen in several ways: they were once in the service themselves; someone close to them was in the service; or they only know what they have seen and heard in the media and are curious to find out more about service life. Of course, if a person in the service sees another service person hitchhiking, they are very likely to pick them up. During the Vietnam War era, many enlisted men were picked up by persons who wanted to know details about service life and what the true feelings of the service man or woman were about America's involvement in Southeast Asia. Even if the civilians called the service person a "war monger" or a "baby killer", most of them were willing to listen to the views of the military person and why they were in the service. Mixed in with the information about service life were, many times, "tall tales" and outright lies told by the servicemen. This is part of the entertainment that one feels one has to provide to the person or persons who picks you up, and I confess having been guilty of this many times in the course of my travels.

Along with the thousands of hitchhikers coming onto our highways came those who would do harm, either as hitchhikers or to hitchhikers. The newspapers of the period contain many articles detailing cases of robbery, rape, and murder of hitchhikers. Being out by themselves, without protection from family or friends, they were easy prey for those who looked for easy targets and easy gain. There are cases, of course, where hitchhikers robbed those who picked them up, but these were in the minority. The police reports of most states do not separate crimes concerning hitchhikers from the categories of crimes in which they occurred. So the robbery of a hitchhiker would be reported as a robbery and would not be distinguished from other street crimes committed on the streets of that city or area. It is almost impossible to obtain precise statistics on the number of crimes or the locations where these crimes were committed if one is doing research about hitchhikers.

Perhaps the best study covering hitchhiking during this period was done at the University of Colorado at Denver during the summer of 1974. It was done for the National Science Foundation and is called "*Hitchhiking -- A Viable Addition to a Multimodel Transportation System?*". Many of the crimes were committed on the major interstate highways and were reported to the state police. Others were reported to the local law enforcement officials and were not reported in the national media. The Colorado Study mentions a California Highway Patrol report, "*California Crimes and Accidents Associated with Hitchhiking*", from 1974 that concludes that hitchhiking contributed to 0.63% of all crime in California.

Since I will be often mentioning the study done by the University of Colorado at Denver, Center for Urban Transportation Studies, I should provide the purpose and area of the study as outlined by them.

"The purpose of this study was to determine the feasibility of legalizing hitchhiking by reviewing problems associated with the activity and by exploring different methods for management and enforcement. An investigation into public attitude and factors that influence it, economic feasibility of a control system, as well as sociological and legal implications seemed warranted, because, if hitchhiking cannot be eliminated, legalization or control may reduce the undesirable aspects and enhance hitchhiking as a mode of transportation."

"The research was divided into two general categories. The first, a study of the current status of hitchhiking, was subdivided into legal aspects, traffic safety, personal safety, public attitudes, and the characteristics of those currently picking up hitchhikers and those hitchhiking."

"The second area of study addressed the feasibility of legalizing and controlling hitchhiking. The most important considerations used for evaluating alternatives were community benefits, economics, and implementation problems from the standpoint of both public acceptance and legislative implementation."

Hitchhiking -- A Viable Addition to a Multimodal Transportation System?, University of Colorado at Denver, 1974

With the rapid rise in the number of persons traveling by hitchhiking during the 1960's came a corresponding tightening of the rules and regulations concerning travel on the nation's roads. I have found no federal legislation regarding hitchhiking except a provision in the Code of Federal Regulations prohibiting commercial motor carriers from picking up hitchhikers. Many states either passed legislation concerning the travel of pedestrians on their roads or more strictly enforced the laws that they already had. Most states have rules stating that any pedestrian must face the oncoming traffic if they are walking along the road, which effectively stops someone from hitchhiking. Or their laws state that walking is not allowed on the shoulders of the road. The majority of the laws and regulations are quite vague regarding the definition of the term "shoulders" as it pertains to a roadway. Does the "shoulder" include just the gravel along the road; does it include the grass along the road; and does it include the sidewalk, if any, along the road? These regulations are enforced in various manners by the law enforcement personnel in each area. Some states have laws which forbid any person from soliciting a ride.

The number of persons hitchhiking decreased during the 1980's. This can be inferred by the lack of articles in newspapers and magazines about hitchhiking and by the personal experience of many persons that I have talked to. Most people say that they see fewer hitchhikers on the roads now than they used to. The *New York Times* published an article on April 3, 1988 stating that "...it appears to be in decline across America, a victim of a widespread perception that life on the road is dangerous." Daniel H. Garrison, a professor at Northwestern University in Evanston, Illinois, is quoted in the *New York Times* article as saying:

> "It's a curious phenomenon. I think it has something to do with the present state of conservatism. People are risk-taking a little less. You don't go out there unless you're confident you're going to be picked up by someone safe."
> "I see fewer and fewer people out there and it saddens me. I see it as part of the closing up of American society. America has fewer and fewer places where people can get together in an unstructured place and talk to each other."

I would attribute this decline in hitchhiking partly to the improving economy which provides more opportunities for persons to own automobiles. When you own a car, you do not hitchhike unless you have mechanical problems with it. However, I have known several college students who own automobiles and still hitchhike to and from college classes in order to save money. Or they may form informal car pools with others in order for everyone to save time, money, and wear and tear on all of the automobiles. If there is another prolonged downturn in our economy, the number of people who can not afford cars will increase and they will surely turn to hitchhiking. The number of bus stations has declined by half in this country in the last twenty years, mostly in rural areas, and this may also lead to an increase in the number of hitchhikers.

The action of most Americans in hard times, according to my findings, has been that when they do not have much in the way of earthly goods, it is easy for them to help another unfortunate person. When times and their fortunes improve, they tend not to make as much of a personal sacrifice. They will contribute to causes, work in their local neighborhoods for improvements, but will not usually take a stranger into their lives and help him or her. In the course of extreme emergencies, yes, but in their day-to-day lives, no. I have seen this by my personal experiences hitchhiking in the slow-economy years of the late 1970's and in the boom 1980's.

But the main reason for the decline in hitchhiking in the last decade is, I believe, the growing sense of alienation within our society, the sense that we are isolated from most, if not all sectors of our society. This may have come about with the decline of the traditional extended family upbringing that was common until the 1950's and 1960's, or the decline of a sense of neighborhood that used to be prevalent throughout America. Is it a coincidence that most reported crimes against hitchhikers happen near large cities, where most persons have no sense of belonging to any family, group, or neighborhood? I think not. The high mobility rate of families and individuals within our society brings about a sense of not belonging to or being attached to any positive social structure such as a neighborhood or civic group.

Migrant farm workers and their families would fall into this strata of "non-attached" groups in America. It was, therefore, with great pleasure that I came across an article in the *New York Times* on July 16, 1987 that spoke of a summer tutorial program for children of migrant farm workers in 11 Vermont schools. The children sent out 2 purple calves, made out of plywood, to hitchhike around the U.S. to other summer programs for children of migrant workers. The calves had signs on the front stating their destinations; an explanation of what they are, where they came from and where they are trying to go on the back. They also carried preaddressed postcards so that drivers may tell the children in Vermont where they picked the calf up and where they left it off. With this information, the children were writing stories about the calves and learning about geography, math, and writing. It is heartening to see hitchhiking, which normally is viewed in such a negative manner, being used as a positive learning tool. I have heard nothing more of this experiment since this 1987 article and am interested in finding out what the results were and if projects like this are still being done.

An article in the July 9, 1991 issue of the *New York Times* details a informal hitchhiking/car pool movement that has developed in Oakland, California. Commuters gather underneath a highway overpass near the San Francisco-Oakland Bay Bridge and drivers pick them up. With three or more people inside, the car is allowed to use the car pool lanes and does not have to pay the rush hour bridge toll. The city and state authorities have cooperated to the extent of designating areas for drivers to pick up passengers, according to the article, which also states that the Oakland Police Department knows of no complaints about it. I certainly am glad to hear hitchhiking being spoken of in such a positive manner by one of this nation's premier newspapers.

The following quotations speak of the helpfulness of the motorist toward the hitchhiker. Notice the dates of the quotes. I wonder if most hitchhikers traveling nowadays find the same generosity and openness among the drivers who pick them up.

> "Unquestionably, the motorist is motivated to stop for a hitchhiker out of a desire to be helpful. This is supported by the data collected in the General Survey in which helpfulness was the most popular motivation for stopping, with a mean score of 4.5 out of a possible 5.0. Hitchhiking is a form of pro-social behavior, and this is a prime justification for encouraging it.
>
> Altruistic behavior, especially toward strangers, is a less than frequent experience in the 20th century. If this is the most common reason why drivers pickup hitchhikers, why should the state prohibit people from helping others? Promoting altruistic behavior is far from irrational, yet state and local governments restrict hitchhiking, and this motivation is thwarted.
>
> Scholars and laymen agree that one characteristic that exists in present day society is alienation, a condition of isolation from others. As simplistic as it may appear, hitchhikers, and drivers who pick them up, are showing that they are not fearful, suspicious, or totally distrustful of others. The hitchhiking situation offers an opportunity for personal contact communication, and interaction. And, is this not a good thing?"

*Hitchhiking -- A Viable Addition to a Multimodal
Transportation System?*, University of Colorado
at Denver, 1974

"He said that he had come to the decision that, compared to
Switzerland, the United States has bad food, slow mail, dirty towns and
cities, and inefficient garbage collection. What is more, according to the
tourist, Americans in general are thoroughly uninformed on foreign
affairs."

"Mr. Lehmann also was upset about a number of other things in this
country - including what he called antiquated open-air telephone wires
cluttering up the San Francisco scene. But he was happy to learn that
Americans are the "opposite of suspicious," and very generous."

"He said that he never had trouble getting a ride, and that the
numerous Americans who took him into their homes "never asked for my
passport or papers and never locked anything up."

"Swiss, 26, Hitchhikes 19,000 Miles in U,S.",
New York Times, November 10, 1956.
Copyright 1956 by The New York Times Company.
Reprinted by permission.

"The Shmoo, it was explained to us, is an animal native to the
American comic strips, notable for its eagerness and ability to supply
everyone with all the food and other assistance he may require -- a sort
of animated cornucopia. The clocks were fashioned in the shape of
Shmoos, which somewhat resemble exaggerated tenpins with feet. Our
experiences in America have led us to regard the Shmoo as the animal
most symbolic of the United States."

"We Saw America on $20.00",
Saturday Evening Post, March 11, 1950

"But quite aside from the mutual faith it bespeaks, it has a cultural
value well worth preserving. It gives continuity to the tradition of
good-fellowship among travelers; and an automobile journey from San
Francisco to New York or from Chicago to New Orleans, with a different
hitch-hiker in each state, might be quite as rich in tales as Chaucer's
classic journey from Southwark to Canterbury."

The Nation Magazine, September 14, 1932;
The Nation Company, Inc., Copyright 1932.

"From Whitman to Steinbeck to Kerouac, and beyond to the restless
broods of the seventies, the American road has represented choice,

escape, opportunity, a way to somewhere else. However illusionary, the road was freedom, and the freest way to ride the road was hitchhiking."

> *Even Cowgirls Get The Blues*,
> Tom Robbins, 1976

HITCHHIKING AS PORTRAYED IN THE MEDIA: NEWSPAPERS, MAGAZINES, BOOKS, MOVIES, TELEVISION

AT&T ran an advertisement in *OMNI* magazine of November 1989 showing a crouched-over person on roller skates. It asks "What can get you across the U.S. for less than $3?" The choices are: "Your thumb."; "A strong tailwind."; and "A 10-minute AT&T Long Distance call, anytime, anywhere.*" The asterisk refers to the limitations "Dialed direct out-of-state, excluding Alaska and Hawaii. Add applicable taxes and surcharges." The ad doesn't mention the limitations on the other two modes of travel.

Friday, January 20, 1989. The *Daily News* of New York City published a photo of George W. Bush, son of the President-elect, hitchhiking a ride home after jogging the day before. Did he get a cramp? Did he jog too far and couldn't jog back home again? Is he lazy? Inquiring minds want to know.

Money Magazine in March 1981 ran an advertisement for the Kohler "San Raphael Water-Guard, a gracefully designed one-piece toilet". It shows a picture of the toilet sitting on the yellow line of a two-lane road running through a desert landscape. In the background is a blonde woman wearing a satiny gown and carrying a bag of the same satiny material hitchhiking. The ad states "At the edge of your imagination, a journey down life's highway takes a surprising turn.". What does the woman have to do with this toilet?

The *Wall Street Journal* ran an National Car Rental ad on June 20, 1985 showing a man carrying a suitcase under his left arm, holding a sign saying "Downtown" in his mouth, and thumbing a ride with his right arm while standing in front of an airport terminal. The headline reads "At Budget, $33 won't even get you out of the airport." Obviously, the man is an inexperienced hitchhiker, or else he is in trouble, because trying to hitchhike at an airport is quite dangerous and the only people who will stop will be the police.

The *Sun-Bulletin* of Binghamton, New York, a late, greatly lamented paper, published a UPI photograph on Tuesday, February 2, 1982 showing a female hitchhiker standing at a snow-covered highway intersection in Detroit. She is carrying a suitcase and on its side, marked in tape, are the letters "FLA". The caption notes that she told the photographer "I'm getting out of this mess".

The *New York Times* had a full page ad on page 41 of Sunday, September 23, 1990 showing a hitchhiker wearing a backpack, carrying a knapsack, and holding a cardboard sign saying "Canada or Bust". The headline underneath says "One way to reach Canada for less than AT&T". Even now, the economical image of hitchhiking sells.

Playboy, in a March 1978 article entitled "Sex On Wheels", shows two young ladies in a Mercedes 300 SL picking up a male hitchhiker. "Here's a new challenge: the hitchhiker, the mysterious, sexy stranger whose outstretched thumb is an invitation to the primal dance." Can you do "It" in a Mercedes 300 SL? Find the issue and turn to page 146 to find out. (Why did this never happen to me?).

A recent Boys & Girls Club advertisement shows a young teen-ager sitting dejectedly by the side of a two-lane road hitchhiking. The ad states "Fact: This year's high school drop-outs will cost America over $240 billion in lost earnings and tax revenues." This infers that all high school drop-outs will end up as unemployed hitchhikers and not live up to their full earning potential. While I totally support the work the Boys & Girls Club is doing, I would suggest that an ad showing a person performing menial labor because they do not have a high school diploma would be more effective.

Forbes's 1991 400 Richest People in America issue, October 21, 1991, makes two mentions of hitchhiking. In the family fortune section, the founder of the Publix Super Markets chain, George Washington Jenkins, traveled to Florida in 1924 by hitchhiking. The Careers column discusses wealthy individuals who are helping inner city kids gain an education and Patrick Taylor, one of these individuals, hitchhiked to Baton Rouge in order to enter college.

Chris Economaki, the acknowledged leader of racing commentators, and editor of the *National Speed Sports News*, hitchhiked in 1951 from New Jersey to Detroit to see the first of what was to become the NASCAR Winston Cup races, according to the October 1991 Car and Driver.

Texas businessman H. Ross Perot said he had great adventures hitchhiking when he was young, according to an edited text of his own words that appeared in the June 29, 1992 issue of *U.S. News and World Report*. He would work most of a summer and hitchhike somewhere for a vacation. He says that he had absolutely no fear about hitchhiking, could get to wherever he wanted to go, and had great adventures.

A few cartoons concerning hitchhiking or hitchhikers:

Playboy	October 1969	page 195
Playboy	November 1969	page 226
Playboy	February 1971	page 219
Playboy	September 1972	page 245
Playboy	June 1974	Party Jokes
OMNI	September 1990	page 71
"Redeye"	Oct. 24, 1982	
"Herman"	July 31, 1984	
"Marvin"	Jan. 21, 1985	
"Beetle Bailey"	July 19, 1987	
"That's Jake"	June 8, 1988	
"Motley's Crew"	Dec. 20, 1988	
"Broom Hilda"	Jan. 30, 1989	
"Broom Hilda"	July 5, 1990	
"Beetle Bailey"	Aug. 20, 1990	
"Doonesbury"	July 12, 1991	
"Beetle Bailey"	March 4, 1992	

Opus, in the comic strip "Bloom County", was hitchhiking in September 1987 outside of Las Vegas and was picked up by a criminal sociopath but since he had a copy of the script, he did a quick rewrite and replaced the sociopath with Zsa Zsa Gabor (circa 1963). However, he left the script in the car and instead of finding himself at Caesar's Palace with Julie Andrews, he ended up lost in the desert, which shows the importance of making sure you never leave anything in the cars you ride in.

A few songs concerning or mentioning hitchhiking (the year they came out is included if I could find it):

"Ding Dong The Witch is Dead"	-1939-	Dorothy Gale and the Munchkins
"Hitchin' A Ride"	-1970-	Vanity Fair
"Crossroads"	-1969-	Cream
"Popeye" ("The Hitchhiker")	-1962-	Chubby Checker
"Hitchhike"	-1963-	Marvin Gaye
"Sweet Hitch-Hiker"	-1971-	Creedence Clearwater Revival
"Big Joe and Phantom 309" -		Red Sovine
"Laurie"	-1965-	Dickey Lee
"Bringing Mary Home"		The Country Gentlemen
"Creeque Alley"	-1967-	The Mamas and The Papas
"Hitch a Ride"		Boston
"Me And Bobby McGee"	-1970- became # 1 -	Janis Joplin
"All I Want to Do Is Make Love to You"		Heart
"Walk on the Wild Side"	-1973-	Lou Reed

The University of Colorado Study, *"Hitchhiking - A Viable Addition to a Multimodal Transportation System?"* reviewed the existing literature in 1974 for the purpose of their study. This is what they found:

"The initial search for existing information revealed that hitchhiking is not usually considered a functional means of transportation in general reference works or transportation reference books. Popular publications tend to highlight the detrimental aspects of hitchhiking: spectacular highway crimes have been recounted to deter potential hitchhikers. A second type of popular literature has an opposite intent--this includes hitchhiking handbooks and articles that encouragehitchhiking and give pointers to ensure a smooth trip. Neither of these types of popular articles wereparticularly useful to this study."

"Most recent literature on hitchhiking presents a negative picture, not only of those who participate, but also of the situation itself. Rarely are there published articles about the many times when both driver and hitchhiker arrive at their destinations safely. The bulk of material contains a bleak and demeaning stereotype of those who hitchhike. The stereotype, like so many generalizations, is neither entirely true or false."

My research since 1974 has shown that this has not changed at all. Why is this so? What are the different ways hitchhikers have been portrayed in the American media? Besides the reporting of events, situations, and crimes that the hitchhiker has been involved in, there are basically nine different images that our media has attached to hitchhikers. They are:

- wanderer
- monster
- escapee
- hard luck victim
- easy sex partner
- victim
- initiator of changes in driver
- initiator of spiritual changes in
  driver
- a person with a sense of freedom
  and adventure

Let's look at each of these images and how they have affected hitchhiking in the United States.

The wandering hitchhiker is the image most common and most comfortable to us all. He, or she, is a person who is traveling to see the country, or to visit friends in another area, or to seek his fortune. The historical images that this image draws upon are the explorers and adventurers that settled this country (Lewis and Clark, Davy Crockett with his cry of "Elbow Room"), the young people who moved west when their towns seemed a bit too calm and civilized (Huckleberry Finn), the persons who left the farms for the big city to seek their fortune ("Horatio Alger" stories) or to go wherever the chances for advancement seemed greatest at the moment (the 1849 Gold Rush miners and the persons looking for work during the Depression of the 1930's). This image contains no malice and can not be a threat to anyone since the hitchhiker is relying upon the public's goodwill. This is the image first introduced by most media who then change it to one of the other "bad" or "victim" images.

The flip side of the wandering hitchhiker is the monster hitchhiker. This monster only exists to do violence and damage to any and all that he or she comes in contact with. The 1986 movie *The Hitcher* shows only this image, a person hitchhiking who kills and mutilates the persons who pick him up. This is a useful image to those who would scare others into not picking up hitchhikers at all. Jan Harold Brunvand, in his book *The Choking Doberman and Other "New" Urban Legends,* tells the often repeated but unsubstantiated folk tale of a person picking up a lady hitchhiker and then noticing by some means (extra hairy forearms or husky voice) that the "woman" is a man. When the woman is put out or tricked out of the car, an axe or hatchet is found.

The escapee hitchhiker is another image. This is a person who is escaping from a crime or from an unpleasant situation such as a cruel marriage or home. Usually the hitchhiker is shown as young, and escaping an unjust situation. If it is a crime, the hitchhiker is innocent and is looking for a way to prove their innocence while staying away from the police. Dr. Richard Kimble on the television show *The Fugitive* is a good example of this. If escaping from a marriage, the hitchhiker was the marriage partner who was beaten or cheated upon; if from an unpleasant home, one or both of the parents were alcoholic or child abusers. This hitchhiker image appeals to the "help the underdog" sense of justice or the maternal/paternal instincts most of us have.

A victim of hard luck is another image that is sometimes shown. This hard luck could be the loss of employment, the breaking down of a car, a missed travel connection, or something else that is not the fault of the hitchhiker. Several auto service centers have used an image of a person in their advertisements who does not do adequate mainte-nance on their car and ends up having to hitchhike, thus playing on our fears and embarrassment about hitchhiking. David Banner, the lead character in the television show *The Incredible Hulk,* is a fine example of this. He was exposed to an overdose of gamma rays which caused him to turn into a large, green, brutish man when he was angered. This green man reacted to most threatening situations with violence towards those who would harm him or his friends. This change was not under Banner's control and so he was a victim of circumstances. Since we have all been victims of circumstances or bad luck at times, we can all sympathize with this image. David Banner was usually shown at the beginning and the end of each show hitchhiking. Since each change into the Hulk caused whatever clothes David was wearing to split apart (except for his pants at the waistline, showing he and the Hulk had the same size waist), I have always wondered how he managed to acquire another set of clothes by the end of the show.

A hitchhiker who will conveniently consent to or initiate sex is another popular image of hitchhikers throughout our media. As is mentioned in the section on women hitchhikers, the thought is that a person willing to place themselves in the public's trust by hitchhiking is likely to have lower moral standards than other people. This image appeals to our desire for sex without any restrictions or binding relationships. Many of the stories containing hitchhikers written during the Sixties and Seventies contain this image and the two films directed by Fred Halsted (*L. A. Plays Itself* and *Truck It*), deal with this image exclusively. It is an image popular in the media but not very truthful to the reality.

How many times have you seen on television or in the movies a hitchhiker, usually a woman, get into someone's car and then get robbed, raped or killed? This is the image of the hitchhiker as victim. Out on the roads by themselves, out of contact with family and friends, willing to trust almost anyone for a ride, a stranger in that area; such circumstances make it easy to portray the hitchhiker as the victim of a crime. This is a favorite scenario in several of the slasher movies I have seen.

Both television shows *Highway to Heaven* and *The Hitchhiker* show the hitchhiker as somehow modifying the life of a person who picks him up. Perhaps the conversation the two of them have starts the driver thinking or questioning his value system or his situation in life. Or perhaps by driving a little bit out of his intended route, something happens which changes the life of the driver. In the movie, *Roadhouse 66*, a driver meets a hitchhiker who helps him fix his car. In doing so, they meet two pretty girls, get involved with the local toughs, and come to face their own personal problems by the end of the film. This is the perfect example of the hitchhiker as an initiator of changes. In the few episodes that I have seen of the two television shows mentioned above, the characters in *Highway to Heaven* are actively involved in the lives and events of the people they meet, while the character in *The Hitchhiker* acts more like Rod Sterling did in *The Twilight Zone*, only appearing at the beginning and end of the episodes to introduce and sum up the action.

Closely related to this image of the hitchhiker initiating changes in the life of the person who picks him up, is the image of the hitchhiker somehow modifying the spiritual life of the driver.   Either by con- versation or by prophetic statements or by mysteriously vanishing from the car, the hitchhiker causes the driver to reevaluate the meaning of his or her life.   This "vanishing hitchhiker" motif has been examined by Jan Harold Brunvand in his three books, *The Vanishing Hitchhiker: American Urban Legends and Their Meanings; The Choking Doberman and Other "New" Urban Legends;* and *The Mexican Pet: More "New" Urban Legends and Some Old Favorites.*   Mr. Brunvand states that this legend circulates in international folklore and has been reported in many countries.   The key elements are that the hitchhiker gives an address by which the driver learns that the hitchhiker is a ghost; a token is left behind to prove the truth of the happening; prophetic statements are sometimes made by the hitchhiker; the occurrence happens on the anniversary of the hitchhiker's death, usually by an auto accident; and further identification is made by a photograph of the deceased hitchhiker.   This legend has been mentioned in song by such artists as Dickey Lee ("Laurie", 1965), The Country Gentlemen ("Bringing Mary Home"), and Red Sovine ("Big Joe and Phantom 409").   In Red Sovine's song, it is the truckdriver, "Big Joe", who is the ghost who gives rides to hitchhikers near the scene of his accident.   In all of these, the message is that the teller of the story will reexamine his life after this strange happening.

The desire for a sense of freedom and adventure has started many persons hitchhiking.   After finishing my undergraduate studies, I just was not ready to settle down into the workaday world.   So I loaded my packs and hitchhiked for several months around the United States, seeing the country, visiting relatives and friends, and looking up buddies from the service.   I was not restricted by any bus, train, or plane schedules and could travel when and where I pleased.   This brought about a sense of independence and control over my actions, which may have been an attraction for many of the young persons who hitchhiked during the 1960's and 70's.   Many drivers will pick you up because they identify with the sense of freedom from life's responsibilities that you show while hitchhiking.   They feel hemmed in by their job and family responsibilities and for that brief time that they share with you, they share in your sense of freedom.   Many young persons have admitted to me the desire to escape from their current situation to travel and see the country and they ask many questions about how to do this. The movie "*The Electric Horseman*" ends with the main character, a cowboy named Sonny Steele, hitchhiking along a 2-lane road somewhere in the West. The camera pulls away from him in a wide sweeping shot showing him alone and free in the American landscape, while Willie Nelson's song "My Heroes Have Always Been Cowboys" plays on the soundtrack. Here, in one beautiful shot, are contained and combined the images of the hitchhiker and the cowboy and the sense of freedom and adventure both represent.

The books that I have found and read that mention hitchhiking use these same images and can be divided into three types. The first group can be called handbooks on hitchhiking. They tell you how to do it and give advice about various states and countries you might travel in. Often the author or authors mix in advice and adventures from their own experiences. In the bibliography, the books by Berg, Buryn and Mines, Coopersmith, DiMaggio, Grimm, Hicks, and Lobo and Links fall into this group.

The second type of book mentions hitchhiking in passing, while talking about the hobo life, traveling, or another subject. The books by Brunvand, Guthrie, Kerouac, Kuralt, Knies, and Least Heat Moon are in this group. James Michener's *The World is My Home* covers hitchhiking quite extensively in the chapter entitled "Travels", as this was how he traveled in his younger years.

The third group uses hitchhiking or a hitchhiker as a fictional device as part of a story. Adams, Michener, and Robbins all do this and do it well in the books mentioned in my bibliography.

These recurring images of hitchhikers affect how the public views and picks up hitchhikers. Rarely, if ever, is an article published or a news story shown on television about a hitchhiker, or a driver who picked up a hitchhiker, reaching their destinations safely. No one would want to pick up a monster or escaped criminal. Certain individuals would pick up victims or easy-sex hitchhikers in order to take advantage of them. But all of these images shown by the media make us think about the consequences of allowing a stranger into our car. No one, so far, has done a movie or television show showing the reality of hitchhiking; the boredom of standing for long periods of time while waiting for a ride; the wide diversity of people encountered by the hitchhiker; the beauty of the country that the hitchhiker passes through; the conversations shared by the drivers and the hitchhiker; the day-to-day fun, grime, and joy of being out on the road. Perhaps with the new lightweight camcorders someone will hitchhike around the United States with one and provide a truer view of life on the road.

I envision a hitchhiker with a camcorder filming car after car approaching and passing by, sometimes interspersed with views of the surrounding landscape. Sometimes a car would stop and the resulting meeting of the strangers would be filmed, with their conversations about hitchhiking, themselves and their lives, the area they are passing through, America and the world scene, recorded, with car and road noise in the background. The end of the meeting would be shown, with the hitchhiking getting out and saying thank you and goodbye to the driver. Or perhaps a group could follow a hitchhiker in his/her travels, filming from a distance as he/she thumbed for rides and following the car that picked him/her up. With a microphone on the hitchhiker, the conversations could be recorded without the nervousness many people show around a recording device. The camera group and the hitchhiker could meet each night and view the footage of the day's travel, deciding what to keep for later use. In this manner, a closer, truer picture of the hitchhiking experience would be obtained.

Marek Gajewski, a Polish journalist based in Warsaw, carried an 8 mm camcorder with him and filmed more then 40 hours of videotape as he hitchhiked rides on private airplanes in the U.S. He spent two months traveling to such places as Kitty Hawk, North Carolina; Oshkosh, Wisconsin (for the Oshkosh Fly-In); Latrobe, Pennsylvania; and Teterboro, New Jersey; as well as many major city airports. He states, in *Video* magazine of October 1991, that his video bag weighed 30 pounds, but enabled him to preserve unforgettable memories of this country and it's people.

The University of Colorado study surveyed a segment of the Denver area's general public to find if a stereotype of hitchhikers existed. The persons interviewed were given a list of 12 adjectives (8 negative and 4 positive), and asked to state which ones corresponded to their image of hitchhikers. 75% of the persons interviewed said that hitchhikers were friendly and adventurous, 56% said that they were transient, 44% said that they thought hitchhikers were area residents and 43% said they thought hitchhikers were poor. No other adjective received more then a 40% response from the public. The Colorado study concluded that since the negative or positive adjectives were not grouped together in terms of response, the Denver public has no set stereotype of hitchhikers. My research shows that this is true of most of America and only the local publication of negative articles concerning hitchhiking brings about a temporary negative image of hitchhikers in that area.

In the early 1970's, a friend of mine had a blacklight poster showing a hitchhiker standing on a road in the middle of a desert, his arm and thumb upraised, while hovering over him is a UFO. I always thought that this was a classic poster which showed the adventurous spirit of the hitchhiker and I wish I could find a copy of it.

This is a chart showing the number of articles relating to hitchhiking that appeared in each of these years in the *Reader's Guide to Periodical Literature* or the *New York Times Index*. These numbers can be misleading. For example, in 1986, the three articles that were noted in the Reader's Guide were movie reviews of the movie "*The Hitcher*". A large number of articles that were indexed in The New York Times related to crimes in which a hitchhiker was involved in some way and the crime, and the subsequent arrest, trial and conviction, all might receive a mention in an article, and all of those articles would be counted as separate items. However, showing this information in this form can give you an idea of the media's reporting on hitchhiking. Does this show that hitchhiking is more dangerous now then it used to be? There is no way of knowing. The chart shows hitchhiking being mentioned in articles but larger numbers might be a function of wider coverage of news then an increase of crimes by or against hitchhikers. It would be interesting to gather this sort of information using all of the major metropolitan area newspapers.

Year	Reader's Guide to Periodical Literature	New York Times Index	Year	Reader's Guide to Periodical Literature	New York Times Index
1926		xxx	1959	x	x
1927		xxxxxxxx	1960		xxx
1928	xxx	xxx	1961	x	xx
1929		xxxx	1962		
1930	x	xxxxxxxx	1963		
1931	xx	xx	1964	xx	xxx
1932	x	xx	1965		
1933		xxx	1966	xx	x
1934	x	xxx	1967		x
1935		xxxxxxxxxx	1968		x
1936		xxxxxxxxxx	1969	x	
1937	x	xxxxxx	1970	xx	xxxxxxx
1938	x	xxx	1971	xx	xxxxxxxxx
1939	xx	xxxxx	1972	xxxx	xxxxxxxxxxxx
1940		xxx	1973	xxxxxx	xxxxxxxxxxxx
1941	xx		1974	xxxxx	xxxxxxx
1942		xxxxxx	1975	x	xxxxxxxxxx
1943		xx	1976		xxx
1944		xxx	1977	x	xxxxx
1945		x	1978	x	xx
1946		xxxx	1979	xx	xxxx
1947	x	x	1980	x	xxxxxxxx
1948	xx	x	1981		
1949	xxx	x	1982	x	
1950	xxxx	xx	1983		xxx
1951		xx	1984	x	x
1952		xxx	1985	x	xxxx
1953	xx	xxx	1986	xxx	xx
1954		xxx	1987		
1955	xx	xxx	1988		xx
1956		xxxx	1989		
1957	xx	xxxx	1990		
1958		xxx	1991	x	x

This section, indeed this entire book, would be much more representative of how hitchhiking is viewed if I had access to other media sources from around the country, for example, newspapers from cities in the Midwest and on the West Coast. Perhaps in a future edition.

ADVICE FOR THE HITCHHIKER:

WHY HITCHHIKE?

"For those like myself who cannot afford an automobile, hitch-hiking offers the easiest and most economical means of transport between points anywhere in the United States. It is an excellent way to "See America First" and in its enforced contacts with drivers of all classes is highly educational. It involves none of the dirt, discomfort and danger of riding the rods or traveling "blind baggage," though it affords the same freedom of movement and irresponsibility as the life of a hobo in the Jack London epoch. It provides all the fascination of a game of chance in the uncertainty as to whether the next hitch will be four miles or four thousand (I once got a 4,000-mile hitch after sundown in a New Mexico pueblo). And it gives motorists the pleasant feeling of doing a kindness which costs little and serves to relieve the tedium of solitary driving."

"The Art of Hitch-Hiking"
Hugh Hardyman, *The New Republic,*
July 29, 1931

"I had always loved to travel and already had seen a large part of the United States. Several of my trips had been by hitchhiking and this rather unorthodox method of traveling appealed to me. I enjoyed starting out in the morning not knowing where I would be that night, whom I might meet or what I would learn along the way. The challenge of uncertainty, the spark of adventure in every ride, the close contact with all types of people - these enticements far outweighed the delays and minor discomforts in hitchhiking."

"Hitchhiking through forty-eight countries taught me a basic truth about travel which is so simple and obvious, yet is neglected by the great majority of travelers. After the monuments, the museums and the scenery have been seen and admired, the best attraction of each country is its people. The only way to appreciate and understand people, their ideas and their customs, is to live among them. To do this, without actually residing in a foreign country or having relatives or friends there, one must hitchhike. The tourist meets guides and waiters and porters. But the hitchhiker is taken home to eat and sleep, to talk and perhaps argue with family and friends. He gains an insight into how they live and what they think, and it is an experience that cannot be bought."

Walk the Wide World,
Donald Knies, 1958

"Perhaps the greatest charm of tramp-life is the absence of monotony. In Hobo land the face of life is protean - an ever changing phantasmagoria, where the impossible happens and the unexpected jumps out of the bushes at every turn of the road. The hobo never knows what is going to happen the next moment; hence, he lives only in the present moment. He has learned the futility of telic endeavor, and knows the delight of drifting along with the whimsicalities of Chance."

"I became a tramp - well, because of the life that was in me, of the wanderlust in my blood that would not let me rest."   "I went on "The Road" because I couldn't keep away from it; because I hadn't the price of the railroad fare in my jeans; because I was made so that I couldn't work all my life on "one same shift"; because - well, just because it was easier to than not to."

The Road, Jack London, 1907

There are two reasons to hitchhike: to get somewhere, and the traveling itself. I hitchhiked in 1980 from New York to California to attend the wedding of a very good friend. I did not have the money for public transportation and so had to hitchhike. Hitchhiking also is, as Jack London says, "the delight of drifting along with the whimsicalities of Chance". When I set out to travel around the country, there were places and people I wanted to see. But these were only locations I was aiming for and I didn't much care when I got there. If a ride offered to take me to an area I had never been to before, great. The travel was what was important, not the destination. These are the major reasons to hitchhike but there are other minor ones to consider.

Why hitchhike? First, it is inexpensive. As Hugh Hardyman states in *The New Republic* article of July 29, 1931, "For those like myself who cannot afford an automobile, hitch-hiking offers the easiest and most economical means of transportation..." The Colorado study showed that the factors of highest importance influencing hitchhikers were "no car available," and "most economical form of transportation" (page 21). As you travel, you pay only for your food and whatever extras you wish to enjoy on your journey but not for any means of transportation such as a car, bus, train, or plane or for any means of lodging if you are planning to sleep wherever you deem safe.

Second, it is fast. Your average traveling speed is that of any vehicle traveling upon the road that you are on and it can be faster. This does not seem to be logical since one would think that the time spent standing soliciting rides would detract from your average speed,but it does not, since generally speaking, a hitchhiker tends to get rides that go faster than the flow of traffic. And if the hitchhiker has a sign naming his or her destination, the tendency is to get longer rides to that destination, thus eliminating several stops and roadside waits. I caught a ride in an E-type Jaguar once that took me through Pennsylvania at speeds over 100 mph and many times I have caught rides with people who seem to pass everything on the road.

Thirdly, it is pleasant, for the most part. You have no worries about running out of gas or of having a flat tire. Let the driver worry about that. You have no worries about having to meet a timetable of events, of having to be somewhere at a certain time, unless you are hitchhiking to an event such as a party or a wedding. Therefore you may relax and enjoy the people you meet and the country you are traveling through. It is a sort of existential lifestyle, free from the restrictions of tickets, timetables, and travel reservations. This is the view that Jack London was expressing.

Fourth, it is one of the best ways to see the country since a hitchhiker can go anywhere there is a road, from the small two-lane blacktops to the large multilane highways that span our country and, if they wish to, hitchhikers may walk away from the roads to explore the fields and forests. You will experience the country in a way that would be impossible with any other form of traveling, except by foot or by horseback.

Fifth, it is an incomparable way to meet people since you will be picked up by a great cross-section of the social strata in this country. Many drivers who pick you up have hitchhiked themselves and identify with what you are doing. Others want to play "host" for you while you are in their "territory" and show you all of the interesting sights of the local area. Still others wish to share in the freedom that hitchhikers represent. And of course, many simply seek companionship. I have been picked up by retired airline pilots driving large Cadillacs, bearded long-haired "hippies" in VW micro-buses, nurses, auto mechanics, ranchers, computer technicians, tractor-trailer drivers, military men and women (both active and retired), college students, policemen (both on and off duty), priests, oil field workers, American Indians (Zuni, Arapaho, Hopi, and others), migrant workers, a tool-n-die maker, a deputy sheriff, high school kids, a interior decorator, hair dresser, construction workers, car repossessor, car salesman, wheat farmer, realtor, musicians, black and white and red and yellow, rich and poor, singles and couples, and just about every other type that inhabits this wide and wonderful country. Tom Grimm speaks of this in the following quote:

> "During one of my U.S. hitchhiking trips I kept a list of everyone who gave me a ride. I think it is a good indication of the types and variety of people who may pick you up. The list includes a minister, lawyer, carpenter, radio announcer, barber, electrical engineer, female schoolteacher, doctor, painter, chemist, newspaperman, judge, farmer, geologist, bank employee, student, housewife, construction worker, taxi driver, photographer, and military serviceman. I also had rides with a policeman, an Indian, a milkman, hotel owner, television cameraman, longshoreman, gardener, lumberman, truck driver, store clerk, forestry worker, post office employee, railroad repairman, shoe salesman, and some Girl Scouts."
>
> *The Hitchhiker's Handbook,*
> Tom Grimm, 1970

I received many job offers while on my travels and a few of them that I remember are: working in a meat cutting plant, cash register repairman, gas station attendant, cowboy, farmhand, heavy farm vehicle salesman, truck driver, oil field worker, construction worker, and automotive salesman. It might have been interesting to take one of these jobs for a while and learn about the people and the area in which I was to work, but I either didn't need the money at that time or wanted to move on and visit other friends and areas.

There is always the unexpected on the road. You can meet and make new friends, meet old ones, get picked up by persons from your home town or state, discover that the driver went to the same college that you did or served in the same Army unit that you were in, and if not, he or she will know someone who did because, after all, it is a mighty small world. Traveling in this manner, you place yourself outside the normal pressures and worries of travel. You have no car worries since you have no car, you have no worries about making a travel connection since all of your ride connections are made for you.

Finally, it is the best way to get to know yourself as an individual. You have a great deal of time in which to think about and discuss all aspects of your life and of the society in which you live. Being out on your own brings out strengths in your character that you did not know that you had and it will quickly expose those weaknesses which you must fight against.

Now let's look at some reasons why you might not hitchhike. If you own a car, or have access to the use of one, you would be unlikely to hitchhike. That is understandable since the car gives you a great deal of convenience to travel or perform errands without waiting for rides. If you have access to public transportation and can afford it, you will be unlikely to hitchhike for the same reasons. Perhaps you are fearful of causing a traffic hazard while hitchhiking or of being in an accident while hitchhiking. Well, if you are driving a car or riding in public transportation, these things may still happen. But the main reasons why more people do not hitchhike are that they are afraid of the possibility of crime or of getting into a car with a stranger. This is a sad commentary on the state of our nation when individuals are afraid to meet other persons. There is always the possibility of crime occurring in our lives and with a medium amount of concern, foresight, and safety, everyone can lessen the chances of it occurring to them. If your first impression of a person brings about an uneasy feeling, just don't get into the car.

Ask around for advice. Mention to your parents, friends, co-workers, or the people you work with that you are reading a book on hitchhiking. You don't have to say that you are thinking about trying it, you might only get negative comments. Ask if anyone has ever done it and what they did, where they went, who they met and what adventures they had.

"If a man can keep alert and imaginative, an error is a possibility, a chance at something new; to him, wandering and wondering are part of the same process, and he is most in error, whenever he quits exploring."

Blue Highways,
William Least Heat Moon, 1982

"To the hitchhiker himself there is one final word. Hold your head high
- not arrogantly, but proudly. The road develops characteristics in you which
are requisites for entrance into business and professional life. If you are
impatient, it teaches you to wait. If you have a temper, it gives you a placid
nature. If you are selfish, it teaches you to be generous. If you are
impetuous, it forces you to think."

> "Thumb Fun"
> Samuel D. Zeidman, *Review of Reviews,*
> April 1937

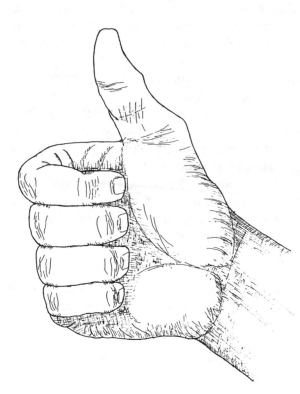

PLANNING YOUR TRIP

"I knew there really was something mystical about the lone traveler with a pack on his back. It was as old as history. In the Middle Ages, monks and people of the Church used to go on long pilgrimages alone. For thousands of miles they would walk, and people always took care of them. The magic those monks had known was still alive. Even in this sophisticated age of technology, there was still compassion for the lone traveler seeking nothing more than knowledge and friendship."

Worldwalk,
Steven M. Newman, 1989

The type of trip that you desire will greatly affect the planning of your trip, the amount of forethought that should go into it and the amount of provisions and baggage that you will be taking along. Hitchhiking trips can be placed into one of three categories:

(1)   you are taking a trip less than a day in length, say, hitchhiking to work or to a college class;

(2)   you wish to get to a place quickly and directly, and the trip will take you more than one day; and

(3)   you are traveling with a loose itinerary of destinations and times but you are willing to let the rides take you where they may if it sounds interesting or fun.

In cases 2 and 3, your planning should be a bit more thorough than in case 1. For example, a serviceman hitchhiking home for a weekend of fun with friends would be in class 2 since he wants to get home as soon and as fast as possible. When I traveled around the States for several months after college, I wanted to visit friends and relatives in certain places but there were no time constraints on when I got there, so it was a class 3 hitchhike.

If you are planning to travel to see the country, and have only a loose idea of destinations, spend some time with an atlas or with state maps to find interesting places to stop and see while you are traveling.

Ask your friends and neighbors if anyone has suggestions on places to go. Your local library has a section of travel books which will give you loads of information on each state and places you might want to see in them. The librarians will be glad to help you. During the Depression, the government hired writers from each state to put together a book of information on that state. These series of books, called the *Writer's Program of the Works Projects Administration (W.P.A.) Guides to the States,* are quite informative and perhaps the most comprehensive account of the United States ever published. They contain geographical and historical information on each state. Read them if you can find them.

The types of roads that you choose to travel upon will definitely affect your ride chances and the speed that you will be traveling, and therefore should be chosen with some degree of forethought. After you decide where you will be traveling, spend some time with an atlas or state maps of the area to see what roads are available. Generally speaking, the chances for rides and faster travel will be greater upon the system of interstate highways that crisscross our nation, than on the local 2-lane roads. There is usually more traffic on the highways, a greater average rate of speed since they are rarely slowed down by local speed zones, and more travelers going for longer distances. All of which add up to more chances for swifter, longer rides. However, to see more of our rural and urban America, the local roads will provide vistas unparalleled by the highways. One of my male friends with hitchhiking experience says that you will meet more women when hitchhiking on the local roads. I'm not sure about that, but I believe more interesting experiences await you traveling on the local roads.

Weather is a very important factor to consider when you are planning any trip since the time of year greatly affects road conditions and therefore your ride chances and your speed of travel. Weather and climate will also determine what extra cold weather gear you should pack along. It is not pleasant to stand for 2 1/2 hours in the rain and snow of western Pennsylvania or in Donner Pass, California in March: I speak from experience. Oh yes, you will find yourself complaining about the extra weight of that sleeping bag, poncho, or ground cloth at times, but there will come moments, usually at the end of the day when you crawl inside it, that make that sleeping bag a comfort you wouldn't trade for anything.

The time of day that you are hitchhiking does affect your chances of getting rides. It seems that near meal times there will be a great number of vehicles leaving the highways to get something to eat and then returning to the highways to resume travel. They usually won't pick you up when they are going towards food, but after they are full and happy, they are more likely to pick you up as they are driving back onto the road. In the morning, the people who are driving short distances to work might not pick you up since they just want to get to work and grab a cup of coffee and read the paper. If they have just started a long trip, they will be more likely to give you a ride. In the evening, the ones going home to work are happy to be out of work and are more likely to stop. The ones traveling longer distances, such as truck drivers or salesmen, might want company for the evening. Many times I have been picked up in the evening or late at night because the driver wanted company to help them stay awake. Friday and Sunday afternoons and evenings are prime time for hitchhiking because many people are on the road for the weekend's travel.

In essence: decide what you want to accomplish and where you want to go on your trip; view maps of the area (buy a road atlas to take with you); consider the weather you are likely to find during the time of your trip; and then, plan your gear around these factors.

ALONE OR WITH A FRIEND

Traveling with a companion as compared to traveling by yourself will have a great impact on the type and number of rides you will receive. Many drivers have mentioned to me they will pick up a single person but not two because "they feel uneasy" about it. From the information that I have found and from what other persons have told me, the chances of getting rides are, in decreasing order, best for:

- a couple consisting of a male and female
- two females
- a female by herself
- a male by himself
- two males
- and worst chances of all, any group
  of more than two persons.

" Two is the best number for a hitching team, and for speedy travel one of these, at least, should be a girl. A recent British survey reveals that girls average two days' travel from Paris to Marseille, while boys take twice that long. No wonder mere males conclude ruefully: if you can't beat 'em, join 'em. A girl is usually glad to have a boy along, if only to form a barrier between her and the truck driver as he gropes for the gearshift."

"Rule of Thumb for the Open Road"
Janet Graham, *Sports Illustrated*
June 6, 1966

It is nice to travel with a friend on the road, to share the excitement and pleasures of travel, but the best of friends may get on each other's nerves in the extended high-pressure situation that a road trip may turn out to be. You two may have different desires as to the direction each of you wants to go or when you want to go. One of you may be an early riser, wanting to be up and off at the first light of the day and stop traveling at dusk, and the other may like to sleep in and hitchhike later in the evening or hitchhike all night. Personality traits such as these are the little things that grow into the big areas of disagreement that bring ruin into a trip.

Before you walk out on the shoulder of the road and stick out your thumb with a friend, the two of you should sit down and talk about yourselves and what your hitchhiking trip is to accomplish. Are you day people or night people; are you the type who is interested in everyone that you meet and can converse and get along with almost anyone, or do you prefer to sit quietly and watch people; are you always on time or always late; how much do you hope to see of the country, or do you just want to get from one point to another in the shortest time possible; at the end of the day, do you prefer to sit and enjoy the spot where you are, or do you wish to wander around the area and see what it has to offer; do your relaxations tend towards the active or inactive, being physical or intellectual? All of these character traits should be discussed and analyzed as to how they may affect your traveling together.

I was once considering a hitchhiking trip that would take me to all towns in the United States containing any form of my name, from Daleville, Alabama to Carpenter, Wyoming. This, of course, would be of little interest to anyone else unless they were totally infatuated with me, very silly, or had Dale or Carpenter in their name. This is an example of the sort of reasons for your travels that you must discuss with anyone before they travel with you.

If you are concerned with the possibility of crime while hitchhiking, the 1974 Colorado study on hitchhiking asked hitchhikers if they thought there was a low, medium or high possibility of crimes being committed against a female, male, or a couple hitchhiking together.One hundred percent of the males and 88.9% of the females asked considered crime a low possibility when traveling with a partner. These are the other results from Table 26 on page 152 of the Colorado study. Notice that males think that females have a higher chance of being involved in a crime (32.4%) than do the females themselves (29.6%).

Possibility of Crime by Sex

	male response high - med - low			female response high - med - low		
male alone	2.6	15.8	81.6	3.8	30.8	65.4
female alone	32.4	35.1	32.4	29.6	55.6	14.8
with partner			100.0		11.1	88.9

The best combination for attracting rides is a boy and a girl. This, of course, has advantages and disadvantages. The two of you will be able to make rapport with almost anyone that picks you up and you will be viewed as less harmful then two guys hitchhiking together. You will, however, have to look for rest stops with bathroom facilities for both sexes or the boy can stand guard outside while the girl uses the men's room. I have done this many times. If two guys decide to travel together, you may find it easier to get rides if you split up and plan to meet that night at a point further down the road. But make decisions on other meeting points down the road in case one of you gets a long ride.

I hitchhike by myself. This is mainly to ensure that I can do what I wish to do when I wish to do it. Of course I have joined up with other hitchhikers I have met at roadside or in rides and for the most part, have had no problems. However, I was hitchhiking out of Farmington, New Mexico one morning and met another hitchhiker. We both caught a ride in the back of a pickup truck down to Albuquerque and started to thumb east on Interstate 40. He seemed okay, except that he was highly nervous and talked continuously. After two short rides east, he told me that he was tripping on acid and asked for my help in catching rides back to the East Coast. We caught a ride to Tucumcari, and I was extremely glad that I was going south from there and would not be traveling with him anymore.

WHAT TO TAKE ALONG

"How to Pack

1. Pack what you think are the absolute bare necessities.
2. Take it all for a little hike, preferably on a warm, muggy day.
3. Come back and give it a second thought."

Rule of Thumb,
Paul Coopersmith, 1973

The style of trip that you are contemplating will affect the type and amount of provisions and baggage that you will carry. A person trying to get from one place to another in the shortest amount of time (type 2 trip) would carry less than a person on a leisurely jaunt around the country (type 3 trip), as the type 3 trip person should be prepared for the expected and unexpected happenings along the road.

All of the gear that you take along must fit into the pack or packs that you carry. Most hitchhikers carry a backpack of some sort whereas the traditional hitchhiker of the post-World War Two era carried a suitcase or duffel bag. I have seen persons hitchhiking with suitcases, but I believe packs are better since they leave both hands free and are also more in line with the generally accepted "hitchhiker image" of today. The pack or packs should enable you to get in and out of your rides as quickly and easily as possible since you do not want to delay or inconvenience the driver any more than is necessary. In this case, two smaller packs may be better to take along than one larger one since it would be easier to place two small soft packs (without rigid frames or supports), into a small car than it would be trying to maneuver a large full-frame pack into and out of such a car. Other hitchhikers have not always recommended packs, as the following quote shows.

"It is not wise, though many books recommend it, to carry a pack, for it creates the impression that you want to walk. If you carry a small and light suitcase, you not only look as if you were walking by accident rather than intent, but it also makes it appear that you are traveling a long distance and not just wanting a ride for a few blocks. Moreover, drivers are sorry for a man who has to lug a suitcase and there is something respectable about having baggage with you."

"The Art of Hitch-Hiking"
Hugh Hardyman, *The New Republic*,
July 29, 1931

On one of my trips around the country, I chose to take an old three-quarter size Boy Scout backpack to carry most of my equipment. My photographic equipment and my daily supplies were carried in a smaller day pack which I carried in my hand or threw up on one shoulder while walking. This method enabled me to quickly remove my camera to take pictures and then return it to my pack without removing the larger pack from my back. I strongly advocate carrying a camera. Many 35 mm cameras of today are light, sturdy, cheap and take fine pictures. Many are so simple that all you have to do is take it out, turn it on and take the picture. A camera will enable you to take pictures of times and places and the friendly people that pick you up, so that after the trip, or in years to come, you will be able to recall the memories and stories much easier. If you do this, consider carrying along some preaddressed mailers so that you can mail your exposed film back home for developing.

Hugh Hardyman now gives the most important advice for all hitchhikers: stay clean and neat. By not doing so your chances for getting rides will drop greatly.

"The most essential part of a hitch-hiker's equipment is a razor, toothbrush and soap. In order to get lifts, it is absolutely necessary to keep shaved and clean. It may not be possible to bathe every day, but there are so many rivers and lakes throughout the country that one seldom travels for more than two days without finding a chance to swim. The man who lets his beard grow immediately begins to look tough, and motorists fear they may be slugged on the head if they give him a ride, or that he may be fleasome or lousy and leave some of his vermin in the car. The rest of the equipment for comfortable road travel is simple: ordinary business clothes with a light raincoat, several shirts, suits of underwear, socks, handkerchiefs, a towel, toilet paper, shoe polish and rag, comb, and a small clothes brush."

"The Art of Hitch-Hiking"
Hugh Hardyman, *The New Republic*,
July 29, 1931

What follows is a list of items that are the bare necessities for hitchhiking any long distances or periods of time, by which I mean over one week on the road (a class 3 trip). Variations of it appear in most books on hitchhiking.

        pack or packs
        camping gear *
                sleeping bag
                poncho/ground sheet
                tent
                butane stove
                cooking gear - combination saucepan/frying pan
                        with lid
                mess kit of plate, fork and spoon
                plastic drinking cup
                canteen
                flashlight, small
                compass
                matches - in a waterproof container
                toilet paper - in a Ziploc plastic bag
        clothes - extra shirt, pants, and underwear
                belt
                handkerchiefs
                swimming trunks *
                sweater *
                jacket or coat *
                gloves and hat *
                boots, sneakers, and/or sandals
                socks - several pair each of wool and cotton
                hat - for protection from sun, wind, and rain
        toilet articles *
                towel
                toothbrush and toothpaste
                soap (biodegradable) and soapdish
                soap for clothes
                razor
                deodorant
                comb and/or hairbrush
                nail clippers
                metal pocket mirror
        first aid kit *
                band-aids
                aspirin, prescriptions, antihistamines
                vitamin C
        needles and thread *
        a few plastic bags - Ziploc, to keep things dry *
        a few rubber bands *
        pocket knife

can opener/corkscrew *
sunglasses and an extra pair of prescription ones if
    you wear them
pens, pencils, address book & notebook *
broad tip felt marker (for making signs)
large pad of paper (for making signs)
identification and letters of reference *
maps (a road atlas is best) *
money and money belt *
camera and plenty of film *
watch

* determined by length of trip, weather and location

You can use the plastic bags to put your dirty clothes in to keep them separate from your clean ones until you can wash everything. You might want to carry some clothespins along to hang socks or other items on your pack to dry as you travel along. A piece of nylon rope, 25 feet or so, is also a handy item to carry. If you are not carrying a tent, you can tie the rope between two trees or from one object to another and hang your poncho over it to make a quick tent to get you out of the rain or sun. Be sure to tape the switch on your flashlight so that it doesn't get turned on in your pack. If you think you might need it, add sun tan lotion and insect repellent.

When someone mentions the word "hitchhiker", the majority of people see in their mind's eye the image that the newspapers, television, and the movies have given us. Usually it is a young man who is dressed in sneakers or work boots, blue jeans, a t-shirt or a flannel shirt, and a denim jacket or an old army fatigue jacket, with long hair and his thumb upraised. This image is not too far from the way most hitch-hikers travel because comfort and practicality come first and these clothes fit the bill in that respect. You will be doing a great deal of standing, walking, and sitting so you will wish to dress as comfortably as possible. Also, dressing in this manner will not adversely affect your chances for getting rides since with the advent of a more casual lifestyle in this country, blue jeans and t-shirts are accepted by a wide segment of the population and are looked upon as the casual clothes to wear while traveling. If your clothes are too outlandish or fashionable, you might lose rides.

Once again, let me emphasize that you should adopt a clean-cut, middle-class American look. I wear a beard now but if I went back on the road for any length of time, I would shave it off because doing so would greatly improve my chances of getting rides. I would not wear any of my hippie clothes from the sixties or seventies either. I would dress in blue jeans and a t-shirt or a flannel shirt. I would not wear my hat (unless it was raining or cold) or sunglasses while hitchhiking so the drivers coming along could see my face and eyes. Letting the drivers get a good look at you improves the odds that they will trust you and therefore pick you up. I have heard that people who wear glasses are thought to be less apt to start trouble. Wearing your glasses instead of your contact lenses might be less troublesome while traveling because you won't have to worry about cleaning or storing your contacts every day.

In January 1974, *Science Digest* published a short article detailing research done by David Alcorn, then a Master's candidate in sociology at Brigham Young University. Mr. Alcorn tried hitchhiking dressed as a "hippie" and then as a "straight." The average wait between rides as a straight was 11 minutes while as a hippie he waited an average of 33 minutes between rides. The article states that he hitchhiked 75 rides, 40 as a longhair and 35 as a straight, and he found that straights pick up straights and hippies pick up hippies but that hippies were less liberal about giving rides. He received nine rides from straights while dressed as a hippie but only one ride from hippies while dressed as a straight. Straights, he noted, also gave him a ride because he reminded them of themselves in younger days or of a son or grandson or out of Good Samaritan motives. His summary was that people were more willing to help individuals whose appearance agreed with their own ideas of respectability.

I had to attend a friend's wedding in Los Angeles, California and I was living in upstate New York. Since my financial situation didn't leave any room for extras, I had to hitchhike. I wanted to wear something more formal than my hitchhiking clothes to the wedding, so I packed a suit, a dress shirt, dress socks and shoes, and a tie into a box and sent it to my friend by United Parcel Service. After the wedding, I repacked the items and sent them back home. This relieved me of carrying those items across the country and of the worry that the items would be ruined when I was rained upon. Besides that, I was quite a topic of conversation at the wedding reception as the person who not only hitchhiked across the country for his friend's wedding, but who also mailed his suit out for it.

This idea can be used if you know that you will be out traveling for some time and might run into inclement weather in the latter part of your trip. For example, if you were going to hitchhike down the East coast, across the South, up the West coast and then back across the Northern part of the country, and you were starting in late summer, you might want to mail your long underwear and other cold weather gear to friends on the West coast so as to have them for the trip back through the Northern part of the country when you are likely to run into cold, rain and/or snow. If you don't know any persons in the area that you are going to be passing through, mail them to yourself care of General Delivery at the local Post Office in one of the towns. You will be able to pick them up when you get there. Check first to see how long the Post Office will hold the items. Or perhaps you could contact a friend back home when you get to that area, and your friend could mail out your prepared package.

For my trip out to California, (a class 2 hitchhiking trip), which consisted of one week hitchhiking out there, two weeks there and one week hitchhiking back, this is what I took along. I know that a week to hitch across the country is a great deal of time, but I planned it this way so that the schedule left me a great deal of time for adventures, if any happened to come along.

> 1 pair boots, 1 pair sneakers
> 1 pair blue jeans, 1 pair corduroy
>   pants
> 5 tee-shirts
> 5 pair undershorts
> 4 long sleeve shirts
> 1 sweater and 1 jacket
> 6 pair socks
> 5 handkerchiefs
> 1 athletic supporter
> 2 pair shorts

1 swimsuit
2 belts
1 pair gloves
1 wool hat
poncho
sewing kit and first aid kit
condoms
3 pair of eyeglasses
2 cameras
bath gear
map
address book, notebook and pen

"I bought a wooden-framed, canvas "Yukon pack," better for my purpose than a conventional rucksack. Into it I stuffed about forty-three pounds of gear - two sport shirts, a pair of blue jeans and a pair of khakis, raincoat, leather jacket, wool sweater, a Dacron suit with one nylon shirt and one tie, a pair of shoes, two light short-sleeve shirts, two T shirts, two nylon shorts, six pairs of socks, bathing suit, medical kit, one towel, film maps, canteen, flashlight, and a couple of letters stating that I was an American citizen in good standing. Also my two most valuable possessions: a warm and compact sleeping bag weighing only three and a half pounds and a sturdy pair of hiking boots which lasted me for two years. Knowing that whatever I bought would be carried on my back helped me hold the weight to a minimum."

Walk the Wide World,
Donald Knies, 1958

A sleeping bag is a necessity when you travel out on the road. I carry an old mummy-style military surplus bag which is heavier than the newer ones, but it serves my purposes well. A newer, lighter one will be purchased and used as soon as my budget will allow. The only problem with down sleeping bags is that if they get wet, they lose their insulating ability and become practically useless. I also carry a military poncho which, besides serving as a poncho, can be rigged over the sleeping bag as a tent or placed under it as a ground cloth depending upon the weather. I also carry one of the new survival blankets that reflects most of the heat hitting it and use that as another ground cloth. In the summer you could possibly get along by using two blankets and a ground cloth, or the survival blanket, depending upon where you travel. I have hitchhiked in Montana and Idaho in August where the temperature fell low enough at night that I was glad to be carrying my sleeping bag.

> "I've done a lot of hitchhiking, so consequently I've done a lot of walking."
>
> Jack Flanders

Wear lightweight boots while hitchhiking instead of sneakers. You will be doing more walking than you might think, and sneakers do not provide the support for your ankles and instep that you need, especially if you are carrying a pack. There are plenty of lightweight hiking boots on the market which provide good support and do not weigh much more then sneakers. Besides, the higher tops will keep unwanted things, like mud or gravel, from sliding down onto your feet after you unknowingly step in them. If you bring a pair of sneakers along, wear them when you are staying in a place for a day or more and this will give your boots a chance to air out.

To make sure that you have matches when you need them, purchase a box of strike-anywhere kitchen matches. Break them into lengths so that they will fit in a plastic film can (the type you get when you buy 35 mm film). With the cap on tight, the matches will stay dry in the wettest downpour. I carry one can in my large pack and one in my day pack.

Positively, absolutely, definitely carry a sign. Having a sign will improve your chances for rides. Any person going to or near your destination is more apt to pick you up. You will not be forcing them to go out of their way, which is a prime concern of many drivers. Also it arouses their curiosity about why you are going to that spot. Signs also signal to the driver that you are serious about hitchhiking. They see that you have a definite destination in mind and are not just going a few miles down the road or dawdling about the country. For example, I was on Route 80 just west of Salt Lake City carrying a sign saying "California". A pickup truck gave me a ride about 35 miles down the road. Before I walked across the exit ramp on my way back up to the highway, a car had stopped for me. The driver said that he had seen my California sign, had turned around to pick me up but that the truck had already stopped for me. So when he saw the truck pull off the highway, he also pulled over. This young man was going to Reno, Nevada and decided he needed company on the trip. So I caught a ride of about 500 miles by the simple tactic of having a sign saying where I was going. Ideas and the materials for signs will be covered in the Tactics for Hitchhiking section.

Always carry a map so that you will know where you have been and where you wish to get off up ahead. The map might show you that it would be better to get off an exit or two before where your ride is exiting. The exit might have better chances of catching a ride, a restaurant, or be on the outskirts of a city instead of in the middle of one. I carry a Rand McNally Road Atlas of the U.S., Mexico, and Canada which I have found to be more useful then carrying individual state maps. The state maps take up more space in your pack and I never seem to be able to reach in and pull out the map that I need without pulling out half of the other ones. An atlas or map is also a good way to keep track of the mileage that you have covered so far on your trip. I always jot down the number of rides and the mileage covered each day so I can estimate the speed at which I am traveling. The blank inside cover of the atlas is a good place to do this, and if there is advertising on the inside cover, tape a sheet of paper over it. Also the drivers that you ride with may wish to look at the map to check alternate routes or the mileage to their destination. I am amazed at the number of people who travel without maps. Don't you be one. You may be able to obtain maps of the states at the tourist information stands which you see as you enter many states.

Money is a necessity on the road, although you will be very surprised at how little you can live with. Food will be about your only major expense, but this can be kept low if you shop in supermarkets and don't eat too often in restaurants or fast food places. Make sure you always carry a number of quarters so that you can call back home and reassure the folks that you are safe and well and doing fine. You will also need them when you arrive in a town and are trying to contact the friend you are there to visit (you did write their address and phone numbers [home and work] in the address book you are carrying, didn't you?).

"There is one almost infallible way to find honest food at just prices in blue-highway America: count the wall calendars in a cafe.

No calendar: Same as an interstate pit stop.
One calendar: Preprocessed food assembled in New Jersey.
Two calendars: Only if fish trophies present.
Three calendars: Can't miss on the farm-boy breakfasts.
Four calendars: Try the ho-made pie too.
Five calendars: Keep it under your hat, or they'll franchise."

Blue Highways,
William Least Heat Moon, 1982

During one trip I spent, on average, about $5.00 a day and during my four week trip out to Los Angeles for a wedding and back again, my spending average was $2.73 a day (this was in 1976). Since I know that a great deal of this was spent on beer and other entertainment items, I could have done better if I had been more tight-fisted. Also carrying a bit of money will rid you of any fears you may have of being jailed on a vagrancy charge if a police officer feels so inclined. This will move you out of the "suspicious character, showing no visible means of support" category that a cop might put you in upon first sighting. You may not want to carry all of your money with you in cash. You could change it into money orders or travelers checks that no one but yourself can cash and which are insured against loss or theft. This is what I have done. I split my money into four equal parts and changed three of those into money orders. I mailed one part to friends in California and another part to friends in Florida so I knew that I would have money available to me when I got to that point. In this manner, I had cash available, money orders to change into cash as I needed it, and money waiting for me at two points in my trip. I only carried 20 or 30 dollars cash in my wallet at a time and concealed the rest on me. You could use a money belt but what I did was; fold bills or money orders in half, wrap in two layers of aluminum foil, then place this package in a plastic baggie. Hide the baggie on you or in your pack. If you are wearing boots, place the package on the inside of your ankle in your boot and then lace it up. If your pack is lost or stolen, you still have your money and if you are robbed, you won't lose it unless they take your boots too. You won't notice the extra weight after a short while and the foil will conform to your ankle.

"To avoid being picked up by the police as a vagrant, especially in the South, it is well to carry identification papers of some kind. I have found a letter on official stationery from a Southern Senator wholly satisfactory in this respect."

"The Art of Hitch-Hiking"
Hugh Hardyman, *The New Republic,*
July 29, 1931

Identification of some sort is most definitely needed when you are hitchhiking. You are, sometimes, violating the law by hitchhiking and may be stopped and questioned by some minion of the law and these individuals get mighty suspicious when a person in this society does not carry identifying papers of some sort. Sometimes drivers will ask you for a driver's license or some form of ID before they let you into their car, because they believe that any suspicious character would not show such an item. I have carried a letter of reference that I received from a friend who was working on the student newspaper where I had attended college. This letter stated that the college newspaper had first purchase and publication rights to any pictures and/or articles that resulted from my trip and that this person was willing to vouch for me. This letter legally meant almost nothing, but it gave me an air of legitimacy and purpose and provided a contact if any police officer wished to check me out further.

The only person to ask to see my driver's license during my travels was a woman driving a small pickup truck in Wisconsin. She said that if I had not shown it, she would not have let me into the truck.

Food is a good item to carry along since one can never be sure of having any regular meals or being let off at an exit where one can purchase food. It is easy and inexpensive to purchase items in a supermarket which won't spoil quickly. Apples, oranges, cheese, dried fruit, and nuts are all good items since they won't spoil for a few days, won't crush easily, and are nutritious. The trail mix types of hiking food are also a good bet. A small flask or canteen is a good item to take along to carry water or other fluid to drink. In hot climates remember to avoid sugary fluids such as soft drinks because they will just make you thirstier. Stick with water or unsweetened iced tea. Or pick up the Gatorade-type drinks that quickly replace the fluids you lose. But please, don't litter.

Eating on the road bears some discussion. You don't want to spend a lot of money eating in restaurants. Stay away from the fast-food chains. I think a diner or local restaurant will give you a better deal. Outside of buying your own groceries, breakfast is about the best food bargain there is. Eating a hearty breakfast will keep your energy level high enough to travel all day, even if you miss lunch. You will find restaurants around most road intersections, and if you don't, you can always ask the first ride of the day if they know of a good place where you can eat and get right back on the road. A number of times, people have said that they were in no big hurry and sat and waited for me while I ate. Also, when you walk into a small diner or restaurant with all of your gear, you will find it easy to get into conversation with the people there about what you are doing and where you are going. Ask their advice about getting rides and about interesting things to see or do in that area. You might find yourself getting a ride from someone there. It has happened to me several times.

You may also be able to find food as you travel along. I have nipped oranges out of orchards, watermelons, potatoes, tomatoes, and corn out of farmer's fields and various wild plants that I knew were safe and good to eat. But beware of the karma of stealing food. I purchased a jade ring at a street fair in Chicago during my travels and four days later, as I was stealing corn from a field near Rochester, Minnesota, the ring fell off my finger and was lost. Serves me right for stealing from others.

A first aid and sewing kit will be very helpful in lessening your worries. You can perform minor repairs to yourself and others, and to your equipment and clothing if they get damaged or torn. If you have not taken a first aid course yet, do so right away. Such knowledge is always useful.

A small pocket knife is always handy to have around. I use a nylon knife holder that slides on my belt to carry mine. A folding pocket knife will be less threatening to anyone you are with than if you pull out a sheath type model. Police officers will also feel this way if they find a knife on you. You can always tell them that you use it to cut the cheese you are carrying.

Some quick hints on packing your gear. Place your clothes in large plastic bags before you put them into your pack: pants in one, shirts in another, underwear in a third, and so on. In this way, your clothes won't get wet if you are out in the rain for a while or if you have to open up your pack in the rain. Carry another plastic bag or two for your dirty clothes. They won't soil your clean ones this way. As you pack up your gear each day, place what you might need during the day in the pack last. Usually it will be a jacket or your ground cloth and sleeping bag. Then at night, you just reach in and pull it out with no bother. Place items that you might need during the day into your small pack or into the outside pockets of your big pack, your food into one pocket, your medical kit and flashlight into another, toilet articles (inside a plastic bag) into another. Keep to this routine and you will be able to find something you need just by feel. And you will be searching by feel many times, either in the dark, or when reaching into the back seat of a car. Keep your pen and paper handy in an outside pocket also. Maps should be in your small pack or easily accessible in your large one.

Since the drivers going by will judge you on your appearance, neatness does count while you are hitchhiking. Hair is easier to take care of if it is short. Remember, that is why you are carrying along that comb. In most areas of the country, it won't be hard to find a place to wash. Most rest areas have bathrooms where you can do a quick wash up, and most gas stations will let you use their rest rooms if you ask politely. Shaving can be done quickly at the same time. An electric razor might be easier to carry than a razor and shaving cream, but then you have to worry about finding a place to plug it in. If you are sleeping out somewhere, look for a stream, river or pond. I went skinny dipping in the Tongue River outside of Ashland, Montana in early August. I had not had a bath since leaving Chicago 3 days before and even though it was about 6 am. and the river was a bit nippy, it felt great. After that bath and clean clothes, I was more than ready for breakfast in the town's diner.

I highly recommend *The Complete Walker: The Joys and Techniques of Hiking and Backpacking* by Colin Fletcher as a source of practical information, tips, and hints on what you will need while living out of what you are carrying. Most libraries will have it.

Speaking of books, why not carry one or two paperbacks with you? They are fine for spending a few hours with if you decide to stay in one place for a day, or are sitting out a rainstorm under a bridge or a tree. You can always give them to one of the drivers that pick you up when you are done reading them. Books also are great lead-ins to conversations. If you ask someone you meet what they have read lately, it can give you a good idea of their interests and desires. Then you can mention a book that you have read that is related to that subject or even suggest something totally different to them. When you are in a town and have a chance to read a local newspaper, make sure you do so. This will give you a feel of that area and it's inhabitants, especially if you read personal ads, want ads, obituaries, and the advertisements from the local businesses.

So far I have been discussing items that I believe any serious hitchhiker should carry along on his or her travels. Now I should discuss items that should *not* be carried: the first on this list are illegal drugs of any sort such as marijuana, hashish, hallucinogens, cocaine, and so on. Nothing will get you arrested faster then carrying drugs, except possibly shooting at an officer. Even carrying alcohol in your flask or canteen could get you arrested for having an open container, if that area has an open-container law. In some states the law says that the driver can be arrested if anyone in the car is carrying an open container of alcohol. You will be offered plenty of drugs and alcohol in your travels (at least that is my experience) and you don't need the added worry of carrying them. But beware of accepting such things. You don't want your judgment cloudy while hitchhiking. That way leads to trouble.

I caught a ride with an Air Force sergeant from Columbus, Ohio, where I had been visiting my brother at college, back to North Carolina. He picked up a friend and he directed us to a neighborhood garage where he picked up something in a brown paper bag. We stopped for cans of soft drink and the sergeant's friend added some liquid from the bag to our cans. Needless to say, that moonshine made the drive back delightful but I was awfully glad I wasn't driving.

The reasons cited for not carrying drugs or alcohol also extend to carrying weapons. The small pocket knife that I carry has been overlooked by all officers of the law on those rare occasions when they did ask me to empty my pockets, but I believe anything larger would have been questioned. I have met hitchhikers who told me that they carry cans of Mace, or pepper shakers, and one who even carried firecrackers to toss in the lap of anyone who got too friendly. They all said that the police only looked twice at the items and gently mentioned that the hitchhiker should be careful. I think caution in the rides you choose and the risks you take is the best weapon to use.

I do not take any pets along on my travels mainly because of the logistics and problems of feeding them and finding a place for them to answer the call of nature. Some people will pick up a hitchhiker and their pet because they see a "Huck Finn and his dog" sort of character off to see the world or they are animal lovers, but the vast majority won't because, I believe, of their fear of the animal, or of it soiling their car or of the smell of a wet animal in their car.

> " "I'd love to take off cross country. I like to look at different license plates. But I'd take a dog. You carry a dog?"
> "No dogs, no cats, no budgie birds. It's a one-man campaign to show Americans a person can travel alone without a pet."
> "Cain't travel without a dog!"
> "I like to do things the hard way."
> "Shoot! I'd take me a dog to talk to. And for protection."
> "It isn't traveling to cross the country and talk to your pug instead of people along the way. Besides, being alone on the road makes you ready to meet someone when you stop. You get sociable traveling alone." "
>
> *Blue Highways,*
> William Least Heat Moon, 1982

> "If you have too much luggage, it's hard to hitch. With no bags, maybe you're a bum. With one, you're a traveler. With two or more, you're a pain in the ass."
>
> *The Art and Adventure of Traveling Cheaply,*
> Rick Berg, 1979

WOMEN HITCHHIKERS

" "Aside from everything else, Sissy, I fail to see how you've even survived. My God! A girl, alone, on the roads, for years. And not killed or injured or outraged or taken sick."

"Women are tough and rather coarse. They were built for the raw, crude work of bearing children. You'd be amazed at what they can do when they divert that baby-hatching energy into some other enterprise." "

Even Cowgirls Get The Blues,
Tom Robbins, 1976

"End Coast-Coast Hitch-Hike" Proctor, Vt., Aug. 12 (Associated Press)

"Three sisters, aged 20 to 24, were home today from a transcontinental hitch-hiking trip that gave them a two months' vacation, took them through twenty-eight States and cost them $49 each. Lucille, Anna and Alice L'Herault, equipped with sleeping bags and blankets, left Proctor June 6. In five days they were in Los Angeles. They rode in trucks and limousines and slept in camps and orchards. The longest wait they had for a ride was three hours in the Arizona desert with the mercury at 112."

New York Times, August 13, 1936
Reprinted by permission of Associated Press.

"Hitch-hiking now has Emily Post's nod of approval if (and of course there is an if) it's a woman war worker thumbing a ride from a gentleman motorist - if the gentleman motorist has any gasoline."

"Workers should remember that these 'rides' are not social gatherings and conversation is not necessary. If they must talk, they should stick to impersonal subjects. To suggest that it be the weather and the scenery is not meant to be funny. Talking about their personal concerns to or before strangers would be in very bad taste. Talking about their jobs might give dangerous information."

New York Times, Dec. 23, 1942
Copyright 1942 by The New York Times Company.
Reprinted by permission.

"Then Miss Linda Folkard, who was born in Toronto nineteen years ago and who estimates that she has traveled -- by thumb -- 15,000 miles, arose to be crowned Miss Hitchhiker of 1946. When Harry Slim shouted to ask if, "being a young girl," she ever encountered "trouble with strangers," she replied:

"That's easy. I ask them if they like poetry. Then I recite to them. My own stuff mostly."

I have mixed emotions about the fact that women hitchhike. I believe that humans should not be prevented from doing anything they wish to, as long as it does not bring any harm to any other individual. However, I do know that hitchhiking is apt to be more hazardous for females than males, as crime statistics show.

A two year survey of 5,000 hitchhikers done by caseworkers of the Travelers Aid Association of America, as reported in *The Washington Post* (February 20, 1972), showed that "25 percent of riders were female, except in large urban areas, notably San Francisco and New York, the female percentage was as high as 50 per cent." This was in the heyday of hitchhiking. The same newspaper reported on Monday, April 10, 1972 that "Three hitchhikers have been killed and at least 18 raped in the Washington area since January, 1970." The University of Colorado at Denver study also found that, in their survey of individuals in the Denver area, 25% of those hitchhiking were female.

Newsweek devoted a full page to an article on the "new and still unofficial category of crime -- violence against hitchhikers." in its February 19, 1973 issue. They said:

"Instead of the driver fearing the pickup, it is now the hitchhiker herself who runs by far the greater risk of being robbed, assaulted, abducted, murdered -- or, most likely of all, raped. College areas provide the best hunting grounds for lubricous motorists; Boulder County, Colo., for example, site of the University of Colorado, reported 120 cases of sexual assault last year, nearly half of them with hitchhikers as victims. And the Boston-Cambridge area has been panicked by seven murders of college-age girls in the past six months -- all of them similarly committed and at least three of them beginning with an outstretched thumb."

"The actual extent of anti-hitchhiker violence is a guess, partly because there are no nationwide statistics, partly because few police departments report it under a special category. In addition, police are convinced that the rising number of reported rapes represents only about a third to a half of those that actually take place -- and lesser forms of sexual harassment are commonplace."

"Some women will take nearly any ride, but always mention casually that they have VD; still others rely on Mace, knitting needles or the theory that opening a door wide enough will make almost any driver slow down enough for them to jump out."

I would like to mention here that jumping from any vehicle going at any rate of speed is not a good idea. But if you have to do it, jump in the direction that the vehicle is moving and place your hands on the top of your head with your elbows together in front of you. This will protect your face if you happen to fall on the road or on the shoulder of the road. Myself, I would take my chances in the car rather then jumping out of one traveling at most driving speeds. The driver always has to keep at least one hand on the steering wheel.

But with the proper amount of caution, roughly twice or three times what a male should use, I believe that a female can travel safely in most parts of the United States. Singer Deborah Harry, as quoted in the *New York Post* of Thursday, November 9, 1989, showed what a lack of caution could lead to. She states that she was trying to flag down a cab in New York City in the early 1970s and accepted a ride for a short distance from a man in a small white car. After getting in, she noticed that all the windows were nearly closed leaving only a small opening at the top. She reached down to roll down the window and noticed that there were no window or door handles. She reached out the little opening and opened the door from the outside. The driver, seeing what she was doing, turned a corner quickly and Miss Harry flew out of the car into the street. Watching for such oddities as no door handle on the inside of the door or cars where the driver can control the electric door locks from his side, will make for a much safer trip.

Many women have hitchhiked safely and written about it and their "rules of thumb" are very informative. Janet Graham wrote a highly useful and entertaining article that appeared in the June 6, 1966 issue of *Sports Illustrated*. She wrote about her adventures while hitchhiking in Europe, but the advice she gives is also useful to those who wish to travel in the United States. The following quotes are from that article.

> "Innocent pleasures, but I had to steel myself against the panic of parents, the anguish of aunts, the principles of principals, the blustering of bosses, the fulminations of fiances and the contumely of consuls. Believe me, it's not the hitching that wears you out, it's the heckling."
> "Ignore them all, as so many have done before you. Despite these surly

thumbs-down official judgments, the upraised thumb remains a valid ticket to adventure for uncountable thousands every year. We took to hitchhiking because it is fast, fascinating and free, while admitting that poverty is, in most cases, more of an excuse than a reason. In addition to freedom from fares, hitchhiking offers freedom from schedules (leave when you like, arrive when you may): freedom from possessions (carry what you can, do without the rest), freedom from tedium (endless variety of vehicles and drivers), and freedom from fixed abode (Anywhere, Europe will do nicely as an address)."

"Boys can, if they wish, play solo. But the girl who travels alone, though she may get rides quickly, won't always get them from the most desirable companions. Respectable men will pass her by, fearing she may turn out to be an assault-claiming, blackmailing highwaywoman -- or else a professional bawdy basket, offering rather more in the way of friendly companionship than the average motorist has time for."

"Prudent hitchers should learn to pronounce a few essential phrases in the language of any country they plan to visit. "No, I am not that sort of girl," will do for a start. There are moments in every girl's life when a driver's gestures -- whether searching for a road map, pointing out the landscape, or even changing gear -- become so exploratory as to become personal, and she wants to get out of the car, but fast. After years of experiment I have discovered the perfect formula, which serves equally well for cases of dangerous driving. Just commit the following to memory in several languages: "Sorry, I'm going to throw up."

"Hatpins, pepper pots, pistols, ice skates, umbrellas and tennis rackets are among the defensive weapons carried by cautious female hitchers."

"For every ominous incident one hears 20 about the kindness of drivers who traveled long extra distances to take a hitchhiker to his exact destination or to ensure that he doesn't miss some renowned local wonder -- be it Stonehenge, the Parthenon, the Pyramids, or Angor Wat."

10 Tips To Girl Hikers

1 Take a companion -- or a hatpin.
2 Be neat but not gaudy -- no low-cut blouses.
3 Ask driver first where he's going.
4 If he's tipsy or wolfish, say you are heading elsewhere.
5 Beware the driver who stops when you haven't thumbed.
6 Never accept a ride if your first instinct is against it.
7 Resist attempts to separate you from your hitching partner.
8 Keep your baggage near you for a quick getaway.
9 Know your route, and see that you stay on it.
10 Learn in five languages: "I'm going to throw up."

"Rule of Thumb for the Open Road"
Janet Graham, *Sports Illustrated,*
June 6, 1966

Elise Gould wrote an article based on her experiences hitchhiking which appeared in the February 24, 1980 issue of *The New York Times*. She admits that most of her experience was during the Second World War, a very good time for hitchhikers even considering the gas rationing, but the advice she gives is still valid. It has been slightly edited for space reasons.

1. - Never hitchhike alone. It is bizarre enough for women to hitchhike at all; alone, it would be next to impossible not to be immediately labeled as some kind of nut. Since many average people fear nuts, a typical sampling of drivers who nervelessly pick you up would probably reveal a high percentage of nuts. Like to like, each to his or her own kind, and so forth.

2. - Only get into a car containing one person (the driver). He - it is almost always a he - must, of necessity, devote his main attention, hand and eye, to the road.

3. - Have one person sit in the front seat, tight against the door, while the other sits directly behind the driver. This will make him very nervous. In time, your cheerful banter and intelligent conversation will disarm him and allay his fears.

4. - Be very intelligent, even intellectual. Converse seriously with your friend about, say, the future of literary criticism. Or refer to the dynamics of the role cluster of siblings in effective dyadic interaction among extended kin in the micro-analysis of family processes. Nothing dashes lechery faster than sociology. (Most men are not rapists; they only nurture secret hopes that loose women will one day providentially flop into their laps. If not - well, they are good sports - and so maybe the next time.)

5. - Wear jeans, running shoes, a loosely fitting shirt, and little makeup. You don't want to look desirable. The preferred image is wholesome, trusting but bright, competent and no-nonsense sturdy.

6. - Avoid centers of towns and wooded sections. Stick to no-class parts of town. Too high-class, and you are a threat; too low, and you may look temptingly muggable. (Don't wear your fun fur jacket or your Gloria Vanderbilt jeans, for instance, or carry a cassette recorder.)

7 - Better still, give up the whole idea. Hang gliding might more safely provide the same lump of terror in your throat and the same proud feeling of "I've mastered it" when you, unharmed, survive.

"Some Rules of Thumb for Women on the Move"
Elise Gould, *New York Times*, February 4, 1980.
Copyright 1980 by The New York Times Company.
Reprinted by permission.

Certain other advice may be useful to female (and male) hitchhikers.

● Be wary of drivers who pass you by, then circle the block and return, for they may have more on their minds than driving.

● If you are hitchhiking with another person, male or female, one of you should get into the back seat of the car so that the driver will be a bit more nervous about making any improper advances.

● I would advise against accepting rides from a vehicle if there is more then one person in it. If it is a couple, however, use and trust your instincts.

● If two females are hitchhiking together, never get into a car with more then two men, and be careful doing that.

● Before you get into the car, make a quick visual check to see if it is the type where the driver can lock all the doors from his side. If it is, tell the driver that you prefer to ride with the door unlocked.

● Always sit next to the door and never sit between two men in the car. Tell them that you get a queasy stomach when riding and need to sit next to the window to get the fresh air. Never get into the back seat of a two-door car, sit up front.

● Put your bag or pack on the seat between you and the driver, if possible, to make it harder for the driver to reach over towards you.

● If you get propositioned, tell the guy that you are having your period or that, unfortunately, may have been exposed to the AIDS virus by one of your former lovers and you are still waiting to hear about their test results.

● Always mention that you contact your parents and friends each day and tell them where you are and where you will be heading that day and where you expect to end up. This might give the driver second thoughts about starting something.

● If the driver does start acting suspiciously, or pulls a weapon, stay calm and try to talk him out of his actions. Look around at other cars and wave at them. The last thing the driver wants to do is to attract attention to his actions. Suggest that he drop you off right there or at the next exit. Stay calm, no matter what. Panic will almost always bring about harm to yourself.

If you are carrying some form of protection, such as a knife or mace, any police officer who stops and questions you might be more lenient with you than with a male caught carrying such an item. The prevailing view among many people who see or hear of women hitchhiking is that such women tend to be "morally loose" and put less value on their sexual favors than other women. Such attitudes have led to such rulings as the one reported in *The Washington Post* on Wednesday, July 27, 1977. The article dealt with the reversal of a rape conviction against a California man.

>"Writing for a unanimous Second District Court of Appeals, Justice Lynn D. Comption observed:
>"The lone female hitchhiker in the absence of an emergency, as a practical matter, advises all who pass by that she is willing to enter the vehicle with anyone who stops, and in doing advertises she has less concern for the consequences than the average female...."
>"Under such circumstances, it would not be unreasonable for a man in the position here to believe that the female would consent to sexual relations."
>
>*Washington Post,* July 27, 1977

I would hope that in the intervening years this sexist and unreasonable attitude has changed but according to my research and experience, this is not so. Many individuals place a moral judgment on persons of a certain class or activity. They do not view an individual outside of the characteristics which they ascribe to that class or activity. As the author of the above article, William Raspberry, states it:

>"What may be closer to the mark is that female hitchhikers tend to believe that they can take care of themselves -- that they are capable of sizing up their "rides" in the first place or, in the event that they guess wrong, are quick witted enough to talk their way out of a jam. That may be idiocy, but

it isn't immorality."

Washington Post, July 27, 1977

"...columnist Robert T. Smith of The Minneapolis Tribune recently offered a ride to a young hitchhiker who carried her infant with her as she looked for work.

"There are a lot of us in the same situation," she said. "Besides, you get a lot less trouble with guys with the baby thing."

Mr. Smith asked if she didn't think hitchhiking was dangerous.

"Life is dangerous, mister," she replied."

New York Times, December 26, 1972
Copyright 1972 by The New York Times Company.
Reprinted by permission.

"Never accept rides from strange men, and remember, all men are strange."

graffiti

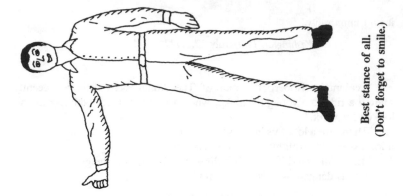

Best stance of all.
(Don't forget to smile.)

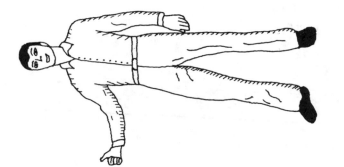

Better: Now people
can see your thumb
is out.

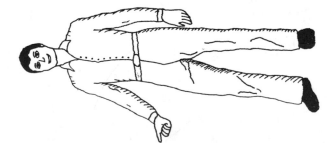

Poor stance.

ON THE ROAD:

A DIFFERENT LIFESTYLE

HOW TO THUMB

"Hitch-hiking appeals strongly to the imaginative young American who wants to see his country as he crosses it and must do his touring cheaply."

New York Times, Sept. 18, 1927. Copyright 1927 by
The New York Times Company. Reprinted by permission.

"The wanderer's danger is to find comfort. A weekend in Shreveport around friends, and security had started to pull me into a warm thrall, to enfold me, to make the wish for the road a craziness. So it was only memory of times in strange places where the scent of the unknown is sharp that drew me on to the highway again."

Blue Highways,
William Least Heat Moon, 1982

"A journey of a thousand miles begins with a single step."
Chinese proverb.

No doubt in your travels you have seen different "thumbing" stances used by different persons to indicate that they are in need of a ride. I believe that a hitchhiker should stand up all the time because sitting on the ground or on the guard rails gives the impression that you are lazy and indifferent about getting a ride. Standing makes you look eager and makes you visible for a much greater distance which gives drivers more time to decide whether to pick you up or not. The three basic stances that I have seen are;

(1) arm hanging by the hitchhiker's side with the thumb out,

(2) elbow bent at a 90 degree angle away from the body with the thumb out,

(3) the arm held straight out from the body with the thumb straight up in the air.

Of these, the third is the best because it is visible from a longer distance and it is almost unmistakable as to what you are doing by the side of the road. And that is exactly what you wish to do while hitchhiking, attract the driver's attention.

While you are standing there requesting a ride, you must exude confidence showing that you know what you are doing and are quite capable of taking care of yourself. Make an effort to establish eye contact with every driver coming your way. Not just eye contact, look directly at the driver while smiling, starting when the car is about 100 yards away and continuing until the car goes past you. This might be hard to do if there is a lot of traffic. In that case, look at the car's driver until he is about 25 yards away and then look at the next car coming along. This lets all the drivers know that you are aware of all of them and of how they are making a conscious decision whether to pick you up or not. Showing confidence in what you are doing will make you a more interesting person in the driver's eyes and will make you more likely to be picked up. If you are on a multi-lane highway, concentrate only on the two lanes closest to you. Anyone in the lanes farthest from you is not likely to pull over to pick you up if there is a lot of traffic in their way.

If you are carrying a sign, the sign performs the function that your thumb would. Hold your sign up across your chest to make it as visible as possible and easier to read. Yes, your arms will get weary, unbelievably weary. I know of no other activity with the possible exception of weight lifting that will tire your arms out as quickly and as thoroughly. If there is a lull in the traffic coming your way, use that opportunity to relax and shake your arms.

The most effective signals that you can send the driver are those that maximize their interest in you while at the same time assuring them of their safety and minimizing the danger that you represent. A sign, a pleasant wholesome appearance, and a smile will do this.

CHOOSING THE SPOT

"For my part, I travel not to go anywhere, but to go."

R.L. Stevenson

"The swiftest traveler is he that goes afoot."

H.D. Thoreau

The first and most obvious thing about hitchhiking is that you won't get rides if you are not seen by the drivers going by. This seems rather simple but far too many hitchhikers stand in places where the drivers can't see them until they are almost on top of them and have no time to decide whether to pick them up or not. Or the hitchhiker will stand in a spot that has no area for the driver to pull to the side of the road safely and therefore makes it much harder for that hitcher to get rides. You should allow an absolute minimum of one hundred to three hundred yards for all traffic coming in your direction to see you. This distance allows drivers to form an opinion of you, to decide if they will pick you up or not, and start moving over to the side of the road to pull off. When picking a stop to stand, put yourself in the driver's place and ask yourself if you would feel safe pulling over at that spot.

Safety comes first in all hitchhiking situations: yours, since you don't want to be bounced around the road by some automobile which is much heavier and harder than your frail body. Stay off to the side of the road so that drivers will not worry about your being in their way and the law enforcement people will be less likely to hassle you as being a hazard to road traffic. I usually stand on the entrance ramp about one-third of the distance from where it joins the main road to where it finally tapers out and set my pack, if I am wearing one, off to the side of the ramp. This varies, of course, with the individual features of how the road is constructed at that spot, but I have found it to be a good rule of thumb (pun intended). What you always have to remember is to give the drivers as much room as possible to get out of the flow of traffic safely and as much room as possible to accelerate to a speed where they can safely reenter the flow of traffic. I repeat, give them plenty of room to pull off because no sane driver will willingly risk his vehicle and his life just to pick up a hitchhiker. And if someone does do a highly dangerous action in order to pick you up, you will want to question their ability to deliver you to your destination safely.

While hitchhiking on the interstate highways, stay near the exit and entrance ramps because police officers will hassle you less there than if you are out in the middle of a long stretch of highway. This also gives the cars more room to pull over to pick you up or let you out and if you get caught in some bad weather, you can get underneath the bridge overpass and get away from some of it. Also you will find more facilities such as gas stations, restaurants, stores, and the like, which you can use for getting food and using the restrooms. There will also be lights at most exits on the highway and these will be helpful if you are hitchhiking in low light situations such as at night, dawn, dusk, or in bad weather.

If you are let out at an exit where there is already someone hitchhiking, say hello and ask how the hitchhiking has been. You might be able to learn about good or bad spots to hitchhike from in the area. I have found that it is best not to offer to hitchhike with another person, as you most likely will decrease your chances of getting a ride. If it is a person of the opposite sex, however, you may wish to consider joining up for safety purposes. This will depend on how the two of you hit it off, of course, and on where each of you are heading. If you are not going to join up, then walk on down the road at least 25 yards before you start to hitchhike as you do not want the drivers to think that the two of you are together, and since the other person was there first, they should be first in line. If the spot does not lend itself to your hitchhiking past where the other individual is standing, then go off the road and sit down and rest until the other person is picked up. If there is another exit down the road, you might consider walking down to it and hitch hiking from that exit. Too many people standing at one exit makes drivers nervous as they do not want to pick up more people than they are comfortable with.

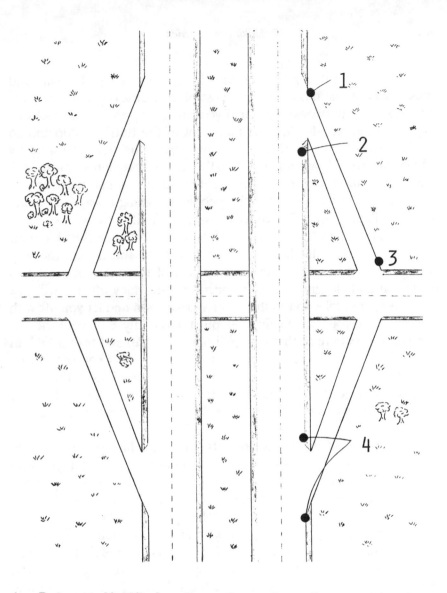

1. **Best spot to hitchhike from.** You can be seen from a distance and there is room for the driver to pull safely off the road.

2. **Okay spot to stand** but the driver has to be concerned with trafic coming up the ramp.

3. **Good spot to stand.** You will rarely get bothered by the police for hitchhiking here.

4. **Very poor places to stand** because there is no room for the driver to pull off the road safely.

If you decide to spend the night here, you can look for sleeping spots in the trees or under the bridge. You can also get away from the weather in those same spots.

I have had rather poor luck hitchhiking in or through towns and cities. I believe that this is because most of the traffic is going only short distances and the people wonder if you are going just a few blocks or a longer distance. Also the fact that a lot of the traffic is stop-and-go worries drivers who wonder if they will upset the flow of traffic by pulling over to pick you up. So I usually walk or take public transportation through the town or city until I get to an area where there are no traffic lights and I assume that the people are going a ways. By doing this you will also get a chance to see what that city or town looks like from close up. Many towns have anti-hitchhiking ordinances within their town limits and by hitchhiking around them or walking all the way through them you relieve the local officers of the worry of having to arrest you and clogging up their court system. Many officers will just pick you up and take you to the other side of town and let you off with a warning. If you are coming up on a large city and your ride is stopping somewhere in that city, pull out your map and take a look at the road system. You may want to have the driver let you out before you get near the city and try to catch a ride around it. Ask the driver about the exit he is taking but don't take his advice as gospel because what many drivers think is a good exit isn't good for catching rides.

Hitchhiking at night has both its good and bad points. You do cover more miles than if you only traveled during the day but you also miss seeing the countryside that you are passing through. If you are trying to make a certain place by a certain time, you might have to travel at night. It is harder to be seen when you hitchhike at night, since many of the highway ramps do not have lights near them to illuminate you. This makes it harder for the driver to form an opinion of you by your appearance and therefore he may not pick you up. Also it is harder for you to form an opinion of the ride that is pulling over and for you to decide if you want to ride with them or not. If there are lights at the exit, you should stand so that the light illuminates your face, not just the top of your head. This allows the drivers to get a better impression of you by showing your face. If there are no lights at the exit, use your flashlight to illuminate yourself and your sign by resting it against your pack so that it shines on you. You might consider wearing something fluorescent or having something on your pack fluorescent if you are going to be traveling at night. I have seen some hitchhikers wearing fluorescent vests such as highway workers or road crossing guards wear. This really makes them stand out in the darkness as the car's lights hit the vest.

The factor of weariness also enters into traveling at night. You might be poorer company for the driver since he may have picked you up to help him stay awake in order to reach his destination. This has happened to me many times, and while the driver may not consider you impolite for falling asleep on him, it is still not a good idea. I recommend, if you feel yourself getting sleepy, to pack it in for the night and find a place to sleep and start out fresh in the morning. It is smart to quit the road a bit early if you find yourself at an exit with a restaurant. You can get yourself supper, a good nights sleep, then go back to for breakfast before you start the day's traveling.

It is not a good idea to hitchhike from rest stops because some people will think that you might have been put out there by another driver because you did not get along with him. You can tell people that the other driver is taking a nap or was taking an exit off the highway that wasn't good for hitchhiking so he left you at the rest stop. You can use the rest stops as good places to rest and wash up while you take a break between rides.

It helps to ask the driver, when they are coming up on the area where they will be letting you off, if they know of any truckstops at any of the exits. Truckers are not supposed to pick up hitchhikers, for insurance reasons, but many of them do so that they will have company. A lot of traffic comes onto the highway from exits where eating and sleeping facilities are available, and it is to your advantage to be at such an entrance ramp. But since these truckers are traveling long distances after eating and refueling, go eat and use the restrooms yourself so that you won't have to ask the driver to stop anytime soon.

I received a good ride from a truckdriver from Phoenix up to Flagstaff and by the oddest coincidence, we were both from the same area back East. He said that right after the war he came West and would never go East again because it was too overcrowded and he didn't like snow. It was dusk when we crested the hills to the west of Flagstaff and saw the beautiful city spread out below, and full dark when the driver let me off and wished me good luck. I walked in the direction that he had pointed me, planning to walk outside of the city and find a place to sleep and resume hitchhiking the next morning. As I walked passed a gas station, a man checking the oil in an old pickup truck looked over and said hello. I said hello back and he asked where I was headed. I said just out to find a place to sleep and then on to Farmington in the morning. He said if I wanted to wait for a few minutes, he would give me a ride down the road a ways. I said sure. His name was Tom and the young lady with him was Annie, and they were taking the truck with it's load of cordwood, down to their ranch outside of Holbrook. They insisted that I come and stay the night at the ranch and they would drop me back off on the highway in the morning. They lived in a small hogan that they had built by the banks of a stream and since there was no room inside, I spread my sleeping bag on top of a picnic table outside. I lay there and gazed up into an infinity of bright stars and thought about all the kind persons who had help me during my travels. For breakfast in the morning, we had eggs from their own chickens, pancakes made from blue Indian corn grown by them covered with jam made from berries growing on their land and herbal tea. They gave me a guided tour of their ranch, pride showing in every word as they talked about the work they had done to earn a living there, and the plans they had for the future. As they gave me a ride back to the highway, I thought again how lucky America was to have people like these and how fortunate I was to have met them. I hope they are doing well.

"Furthermore, we know America, we're at home; i can go anywhere in America and get what i want because it's the same in every corner, i know the people, i know what they do. We give and take and go in the incredibly complicated sweetness zigzagging every side."

Dean Moriarty
On The Road, Jack Kerouac, 1955

"But remember, hassles make the best stories."

The Art and Adventure of Traveling Cheaply,
Rick Berg, 1979

TACTICS FOR HITCHHIKING

"He travels the fastest who travels alone."
R. Kipling

"After a lifetime of travel he settled here on the Costa del Sol and told us there were five rules for successful travel. Never eat in any restaurant called Mom's. Never play poker with anyone called Doc. Get your laundry done at every opportunity. Never refuse sex. And order any dish containing wild rice."

The Drifters, James Michener, 1971

These are tactics that I have found very useful while hitchhiking and desire to pass along to other hitchhikers since it will improve our image and the reception we will receive.

Make eye contact with the driver of every vehicle that is coming your way. This shows that you are a friendly and open person who would be interesting to have along for the ride. If you are standing on a multi-lane highway, concentrate on the closest two lanes of traffic since they are more likely to pick you up. A hitchhiker I admire calls this "the silent salesmanship of the hitchhiker" and declares it all-important for catching rides.

A smile will also show this and it is just about the most important piece of attitude and equipment that you can carry along. More people will pick you up if you have a smile than if you are standing there with a neutral, noncommittal expression or a disgruntled, unhappy face. If you are standing in the midst of a rainstorm or a snowstorm with a smile on your face, people will think either that you are happy to be out traveling no matter what the weather and are a worthwhile person to pick up or are weird enough to be interesting to talk to.

I was just leaving Billings, Montana after getting something to eat and using the facilities at a gas station. I was walking down the entrance ramp to get on the highway and heard a vehicle coming down the ramp behind me so I turned, stuck out my thumb, and smiled. That driver drove me through Yellowstone National Park, bought me lunch, and on to Boise, Idaho and invited me to stay at his ranch. I stayed at his horse ranch for three days, went horseback riding, and saw part of the country around that area with him. I willingly paid for my stay there by helping doing chores around the farm. That man did that for me because, as he told me later, "No one who smiles like you could mean anyone any harm."

If you are walking along a road, either a two-lane road or along a highway to get to a better spot from which to hitchhike, turn completely around if you hear a vehicle coming along and stick out your thumb. Keeping your back to the traffic while sticking out your thumb is impolite and shows that you are not really interested in getting a ride. Also the drivers need to see you in order to make that decision to pick you up.

> "We had already developed some additional theories about hitchhiking. Most American hitchhikers, we noted, simply slumped by the roadway, looking utterly miserable, and waving their thumbs in a languid and dejected manner. Not for us. We smiled, bowed, waved, and gestured vigorously. We discovered in those three fruitless hours that smiling for that length of time could become an excruciating physical effort."
>
> "We Saw America on $20.00"
> William Harvard and Kenneth Cosslett,
> *Saturday Evening Post,* March 11, 1950

A sign will improve your chances of a ride by better than 50 percent. The two persons mentioned in the above quote used a sign that said "English Students Seeing America". A piece of cardboard with the traveler's destination scribbled on it in pen or magic marker is the image of the sign that most people have and while this is better than nothing, cardboard does have its disadvantages. You may not be able to find a piece of cardboard when you need it or you may not be able to find something to write with on the cardboard. The darkness of the cardboard makes it hard to see at night even when you are standing under a streetlight and writing on brown cardboard with black pen just makes it harder to see. Cardboard also has a bad habit of getting soggy and falling apart when it gets wet and it is also not easily folded to stick into your pack when you are getting a ride. On the plus side, it is inexpensive and biodegradable. Personally, I do not use cardboard except as a last resort.

What I do use is a white bath towel. If you fold the bath towel in half along its longer side so you have more of a square shape, and then fold it again, you will have an area that is one-eighth of the towel. If this towel is then pinned together with large safety pins (baby diaper pins work excellently, as a female friend pointed out to me), and you write on this side with a magic marker, you have a sign that is easily seen both day and night. By refolding and repinning the towel, you have a total of eight sides that you can use. I write the words "North", "South", "East", and "West", on four of the sides of my hitchhiking towel and still have four more sides to write more precise destinations upon. I carry a large magic marker in my pack to do this and also to lend to other hitchhikers so that they can make up cardboard signs if they need to. This sign can be stuffed easily into a small area of your pack, which cardboard won't do, and can be used as a pillow, or used to wash and dry your face or shield your head from the sun. The towel can be used after your trip for its original purpose as a bath towel although some of your house guests may question why the towel is written upon if they happen to see it. Then this is the time to regale them with stories of your hitchhiking experiences.

" The Hitchhiker's Guide to the Galaxy has a few things to say on the subject of towels.
A towel, it says, is about the most massively useful thing an interstellar hitchhiker can have. Partly because it has great practical value. You can wrap it around you for warmth as you bound across the cold moons of Jaglan Beta; you can lie on it on the brilliant marble-sanded beaches of Santraginus V, inhaling the heady sea vapors; you can sleep under it beneath the stars which shine so redly on the desert world of Kakrafoon; use it to sail a miniraft down the slow heavy River Moth; wet it for use in hand-to-hand combat; wrap it round your head to ward off noxious fumes or avoid the gaze of the Ravenous Bugblatter Beast of Traal (a mind-bogglingly stupid animal, it assumes that if you can't see it, it can't see you - daft as a brush, but very ravenous); you can wave your towel in emergencies as a distress signal, and of course dry yourself off with it if it still seems clean enough.
More importantly, a towel has immense psychological value. For some reason, if a strag (strag: nonhitchhiker) discovers that a hitchhiker has his towel with him, he will automatically assume that he is also in possession of a toothbrush, washcloth, soap, tin of biscuits, flask, compass, map, ball of string, gnat spray, wet-weather gear, space suit etc., etc. Furthermore, the strag will then happily lend the hitchhiker any of these or a dozen other items

that the hitchhiker might accidentally have "lost". What the strag will think is that any man who can hitch the length and breadth of the Galaxy, rough it, slum it, struggle against terrible odds, win through and still know where his towel is, is clearly a man to be reckoned with."

The Hitchhiker's Guide to the Galaxy,
Douglas Adams, 1979

The popularity of *The Hitchhiker's Guide to the Galaxy* (radio broadcasts, books, and television series) has lead to several articles using "The Hitchhiker's Guide to.." as a lead-in title. *Vax Professional,* a computer magazine, has a regular column called "The Hitchhiker's Guide to VMS:" in which a computer programmer consults a talking book, just like in Douglas Adams's series.

During my college years, as I often hitchhiked from college to my home town and back again, I would stop at my great-uncle's and great-aunt's house to visit. My great-aunt surprised me by making a sign which was heavy cotton material with a piece of plastic sewn inside. It was large enough to write the town names upon and the plastic would prevent rain from coming through. Although I have retired that hitchhiking towel, I still keep it as a fond memento of a fine lady.

Another good sign that I have seen is a large hand made out of Masonite or plywood in which the thumb was hinged to fold down over the palm area of the hand. Folded up like this, it fit easier into the pack. This sign had a strap on its back to make it easier to hold and was painted a day-glow orange that could be seen for miles. This does seem to be rather an extravagant length to go to for a hitchhiking sign but the owner assured me that it does indeed attract attention and gets him rides, which after all, is the object of hitchhiking signs.

Putting slogans on your sign instead of destinations is another way of attracting the driver's attention and thereby getting rides. Some of the slogans and sayings that I have seen or heard of include:

Going Home
Going to see Mom
Just Had a Bath
Good Listener, Good Conversationalist
Albuquerque Please

Oz
I Know a Thousand Jokes
I'm not out to Rob or Mug anyone today
I give Green Stamps
RIDE PLEASE! Male, 24, lonely, discreet, wishes to
meet any sincere driver. willing to go anywhere. can
discuss any topic. sex, age & race no barrier
If you don't give me a ride, I'll vote for Hoover (a common
sign seen in the fall of 1932),
En route to New York to appear on Major Bowes'
program. (common in 1934 and 1935, refers to a very popular
radio amateur hour show)
Nonsmoker

"Finally he found the solution. It was in two parts. The first consisted of
a square foot of polished aluminum, embossed with the college initials.
Clearly visible from afar by day, it catches the glare of approaching headlights
by night, like a road reflector sign. Attached to the side of a suitcase, the sign
proclaims at once that a student wants a lift.

Part two is a booklet, the student member's passport. On the front cover
are his photograph and signature. Inside is pasted a memorandum from his
college office, stamped with the college seal, attesting that he is a student in
good standing. The rest of the booklet is made up of perforated sheets of
cards. As soon as he gets into a stranger's car, a member of Carson's club
presents these credentials and signs one of the perforated cards, which reads:
"I herewith release you of any and all liability due to my having been a
passenger in your automobile." Signed with the student's name and address,
this becomes a legal document and makes an instant hit with motorists."

"Thumbs Across the Continent",
Loring A. Schuler, *Coronet*, May 1941

You can also use your sign to get local information. When you are
in a laundromat, restaurant, or local library (all good places to meet
people and spend time while you are cleaning up or waiting to meet a
friend), if you happen to "just by accident" pull out your sign while
looking for something else, it will catch someone's eye. Then you can
explain what you are doing and ask if there is any places of interest
locally that you should see. This was how I got to see the petrified
watermelons of Idaho.

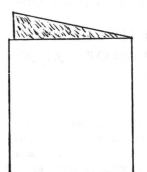

*Fold your white
bath towel in half,*

*and in half again.
Pin the edges with
large safety pins.
Diaper pins work
great.*

*Use marking pens
(wide-tipped ones)
to write your
destination. If
you are planning
a long trip, write
general directions
like this. Use the
other side for
specific cities.*

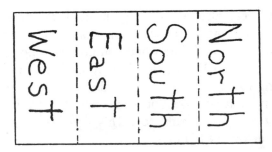

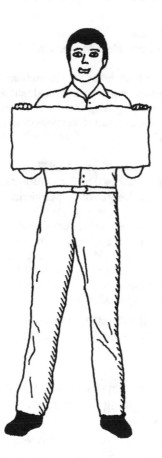

A sign this large really catches everyone's eye and the white towel shows up well at night.

YOU AND THE DRIVER

"Now the first question from a hitchhiker never varies: "How far ya goin'?" "

Blue Highways,
William Least Heat Moon, 1982

"When picked up, the hitch-hiker usually explains where he is going and perhaps why; where he is coming away from and perhaps why; and always he explains what luck he had in getting lifts from others. His daily mileage is variable, depending on an early start, conditions of roads and weather, traffic and other local factors."

New York Times, Sept. 18, 1927
Copyright 1927 by The New York Times
Company. Reprinted by permission.

"The closer I got to Montana, the more miraculous these people seemed. They trusted me, a stranger, and they opened themselves to me. Somehow an affinity developed during every ride, an affinity that grew because I was grateful for their kindness and they were grateful for my concern with their lives. By the time the ride was over, I knew them well; the driver had become a friend. Usually we exchanged addresses."

"On The Road", Michael Shnayerson,
Harper's Magazine, November 1974

The driver is your most important ally when hitchhiking. He or she is the person that will be giving you a ride to move you along toward your destination. But you do not have to accept every ride that stops to pick you up. Common sense and intuition will tell you that if the ride doesn't look good for any reason, you should not get into that vehicle. The first question that most drivers will ask you when they pull over is "Where are you going to?" It is quite all right to say that you are heading West, or South, or North, and then to ask the driver where they are heading. If their answer is vague, or hesitant, take a closer look at the driver and the vehicle. If some sixth sense warns you not to take that ride, you can just say "Thank you, but I believe that I will wait for someone going a bit closer to my destination" or "No thank you, but I think that I will wait for another ride". And if you smell alcohol, marijuana, or see a number of empty beer or liquor bottles near the driver, listen to your intuition and don't get in. Better slow and safe than fast and sorry.

There are many varied reasons as to why you were picked up by the driver. The driver may have wanted company and conversation while driving because it does get boring traveling on the road, especially if they are driving any distance. The driver may have wanted someone to help them stay awake. I have been picked up many times by persons who have said that they had to travel a certain distance that night and it would be easier to stay awake with someone else in the car or truck. The driver may be curious about you and why you are out hitchhiking; where you are from; where you are going; what is it like to be hitch-hiking; how many rides you get in a day; etc., etc. People are always curious about the lifestyle of a hitchhiker and ask questions such as; how do you eat; where do you go to the bathroom; where do you sleep at night; what problems do you have while hitchhiking; do you ever get picked up by bad rides; etc. A great many individuals are sort of jealous of the free lifestyle that a hitchhiker has or seems to possess; the freedom to travel when and where they desire without the handicap of a job or bills or any tightly restricting routine. Many people have said to me, "I wish I could do what you are doing, just travel around and see the country and see people. I wish I could do it, just take off right now and do it".

Once you have accepted a ride, establish in the driver's mind that you are a person with an identity and strings to family, friends, and a destination. This will aid in your safety by making it clear that you are not just some footloose kid wandering around the country. Ask them what they do for a living and relate to that. If they are a student or a family person, ask them about the courses they are taking or about how it is raising a family in that area. Mention that you called your folks last night and you also called the friends that are to meet you later in the day in the city up ahead. Mentioning that you are traveling on a shoestring budget will erase any thoughts that they might have about you carrying a fat wallet. Ignore or squash any talk that is leading into areas that make you uncomfortable, such as sex or drugs. This should enable you to cope with any drivers who might assume that you are out looking for thrills on the roads of America.

Now the driver will be asking you lots of questions about hitch-hiking and you should be able to satisfy his or her curiosity. But what if this is only your first or second hitchhiking experience and you don't want to admit that for some reason? Well, in that case, I hereby give you permission to quote from any and all sections from this book. Or using your knowledge of the area you grew up in, talk about how it is to hitchhike around there. In this manner, you can fake your knowledge, appear quite the worldly sort, and improve the image of the hitchhiker at the same time. But remember to appreciate your audience. You don't want to be telling stories that the driver will sense are falsehoods because that will reflect back on his treatment of you and other hitchhikers.

Of course, once the driver has picked you up, you are under some obligation to him or her. It is best to follow the lead that the driver gives you. If they wish to talk, they will start a conversation and you should join in. Most of the time this will be the case. If they wish to ride in silence, you will notice this by the short answers or no answer to your questions and comments. Usually they want a passenger who is awake and alert and that is your obligation. If they are riding with the radio off and all of the windows rolled up, you should refrain from altering any of these items. Of course, if you feel in need of fresh air for some reason, or need some music to help you stay awake, politely ask. Most drivers I have met were very pleasant people and by exchanging talk and stories about the areas of the country that we knew, left me with memories that I bet are better then most of the pictures that most tourists come back home with.

I was hitchhiking in my army uniform and caught a ride in Virginia with a truck driver who was going all the way to Scranton, Pennsylvania but had some stops to make on the way. So in order to help speed him along, I helped unload cases of frozen broccoli at his stops in Baltimore and Washington. The people at these places thought it was hilarious that a serviceman in uniform was willing to do this but understood my actions. The driver was very thankful and insisted on buying me a meal before we separated and, by asking around at the truckstop, found me a ride heading in my direction.

The University of Colorado at Denver's survey of drivers who pick up or who have picked up hitchhikers brings to light some very interesting information. The main reason people gave for picking up hitchhikers was to be helpful. That's right, to be helpful. The next reason was that the drivers identified with the hitchhiker because the drivers had, sometime in their life, hitchhiked themselves. 69.5% of the drivers had hitchhiked sometime in their lives and 42.6% had hitchhiked during the past two years. The other reasons given were a sense of adventure and wanting companionship.

The reasons drivers gave concerning their decision to pick up a particular hitchhiker were, in descending order: the hitchhiker was at a convenient location; the hitchhiker was readily seen; the physical appearance of the hitchhiker; the hitchhiker was alone; the hitchhiker was of the same age group as the driver; the hitchhiker was carrying a sign; and the sex of the hitchhiker. So by applying these factors, you can dramatically improve your chances of getting a ride.

Why won't drivers pick you up? According to the reasons given in answer to the Colorado survey, personal safety was the main reason. Drivers fear hitchhikers, just as hitchhikers fear drivers. The reasons given were, in descending order: prefer not to pick up a stranger; the driver is likely to be the victim of a crime; the driver was traveling alone; the driver had family or passengers in the car; hitchhiking is illegal; and the driver worried about the probability of causing an accident.

"I pick them up because I am sorry for them. Their appeal is elemental; they are footsore, tired, and hungry, and it's a little thing to let them sit in the car for awhile."

"But chiefly I pick them up because they are amusing and interesting. Strangers have none of the middle ground of talk; there is nothing between the weather and the stuff they live by."

"Whereas it is the man with overmastering interests of his own who makes the way seen short. Give me a crank or a crackpot every time, a fellow who can't wait to get into the car before he starts to expound or argue. Communism or some crazy diet, it's all one with me as long as he is excited about it."

"What a poor thing is safety compared to this."

"I Pick 'Em Up", Bergen Evans,
Scribner's Magazine, February 1939

"What I want to concentrate on here is the reverse process - that is, the benefits for the motorist of picking up hitchhikers. These have primarily to do with energy.   Hitchers have to be great or foolish to be out on the American hiways in the first place, and that already distinguishes them. They have a great deal of energy available to cope with the trials of the road, and when you pick up a hitchhiker you're going to get some of that juice."

> From *Vagabonding in America: A Guidebook About Energy* by Ed Buryn and Stephanie Mines. Copyright 1973 by Ed Buryn. Reprinted by permission of Random House, Inc., and The Bookworks.

Ansley J. Coale of Ukiah, California found out about the benefits of picking up hitchhikers. One day in 1973 he picked up a hitchhiker named Hubert Germain-Robin. Mr. Coale owned acreage in Mendocino County, Mr. Germain-Robin was looking for a place to start a distillery to make brandy. They entered into a partnership and now produce a fine California brandy under the Germain-Robin label. You may read about this in the *New York Times Magazine* of September 4, 1988.

Remember, you are not obligated to accept any and all rides that stop for you. If you stand outside of the car or truck while asking where the driver is going, this will give you time to gather an impression of the person or persons inside and decide if you will accept the ride. Just be polite while you are declining the ride and most of the drivers will not take offense at your refusal. If they do, just pick up your gear and back away from the vehicle and walk toward the oncoming traffic and return to hitchhiking after that car has left. There will be another ride coming along sooner or later that will better suit your purposes. More will be said upon how to handle bad rides or unpleasant situations in the section entitled Road Hassles.

Compatibility is the main goal in getting along with the drivers that give you rides. You will find yourself discussing many subjects from politics to religion, child-raising to drug legalization and one of the worst things to do is to get into an argument with the driver. They may decide to kick you out of their car in the middle of nowhere in bad weather. No matter how fervent your feelings on a subject, discuss it instead of arguing it. One of the reasons you are out on the road is to learn about other people, their lives and feelings and you can't do that while advertising your opinions. Be a listener more than a talker. You won't get bounced out of the car and you may learn the other person's stance on the subject has some good points to it and they may learn the same about your beliefs. If my experiences are any indication of the types of people that pick up hitchhikers, you will be conversing with a great cross-section of this country's social strata and you will have an unrivaled opportunity to learn about how people in this country live, think and feel about the issues of our time and their ideas on how to solve many of the problems facing this country.

Common courtesy is also the best option if you are offered food or drink by the driver while you are traveling. If we are in their vehicle, I always offer to share whatever food I am carrying. If we are in a restaurant or other eating place, I always offer to pay my way, but if the driver insists on paying, I accept their hospitality with thanks. Don't freeload, don't ask or demand that the driver buy you something. This just makes it more uncomfortable to travel with that driver and because of that experience, that driver may not pick up any more hitchhikers.

If the drive is a very long one, you may offer to drive for a while after a decent interval has passed when you and the driver are at ease in each other's company. Be sure however, that you can handle the vehicle. Politeness is nice but don't offer to drive the 18-wheel tractor trailer that just picked you up if this is the first time that you ever sat in one. If the driver does ask you to drive, be aware that the driver will be extremely nervous about a stranger driving his car so be on your best behavior and drive defensively so you can be sure you are not upsetting the driver. I have found that if I drive like I am taking a driver's license road test, and could fail at any moment, the driver relaxes much faster than if I drive their vehicle like I drive my car. Some drivers may ask you if you could drive for awhile, as they are tired, and in this situation, accept and take extreme care of their vehicle.

I was hitchhiking on Route 80 in Pennsylvania, having just left one army buddy's house in Williamsport and heading to see another in Ohio. A new Cadillac came up the ramp where I was standing, slowed, and stopped. A middle-aged man rolled down the window and asked where I was going. After I told him near Canton, Ohio, he said that he could give me a ride at least across Pennsylvania. It turned out that we had both spent the weekend in Williamsport, he visiting his brother and I visiting my army friend. He said he was a retired pilot for Pan-Am and was going to visit friends in Chicago and then going fishing at his place in Idaho. We talked for over an hour and then he asked me if I had a driver's license and could drive for a while. I said yes to both questions. He said that he and his brother had been up late last night and he could use some rest from driving. We stopped and switched places. I put the seat belt on, adjusted the inside and outside rearview mirrors, and then gently pulled out into traffic. We talked and he watched me drive for about a half hour, and then, evidently accepting my driving, he said that he was going to take a short nap. An hour and one-half later, he woke up and asked where we were. Surprised at the answer, he said that he hadn't planned to sleep so long but must have been more tired then he had thought. We crossed into Ohio and left the highway to stop at a restaurant where he bought lunch. Refreshed, we got back on the road. When leaving me off, he thanked me greatly for the help in driving while I thanked him for the ride and lunch.

I was leaving Binghamton, New York and I saw a hitchhiker standing in the rain. The spot where he was standing was on an entrance ramp from one highway to another highway in the midst of the city, a terrible place to stand. I quickly pulled over and picked him up. I had just picked up a cup of coffee for the road and as we shared it, he told me of his travels. He was from Maine and had problems finding work up there so when a friend of his called and offered a truckdriving job in Tennessee, he decided to take it. So he was hitchhiking to Tennessee. We talked about hitchhiking, jobs, his failed marriage, his daughter and children in general, the state of the world, books, and many other things. When we got near where our paths would separate, I invited him in for dinner at a truckstop. He, at first, politely refused and then when I insisted, accepted my offer. While eating I told him of the many occasions when drivers had bought meals for me and said that the only repayment I wanted was for him to do the same for some other hitchhiker when the opportunity came. I drove him back to the highway and let him out, warm, dry, and fed and headed on my way, feeling that I had repaid a small part of a large debt.

ROAD HASSLES AND PROBLEMS

"Now, gentle reader, a word of warning should you ever go on the "road": Always placate the policeman. He is at once the dispenser and obfuscator of life, liberty, and pursuit of happiness. He shapes the destinies of lesser creatures, and free air or dungeon lurk in his gruff "Move on," or "Come on." Placate him by all means, when your trails cross, and one way to do this is to arouse his interest."

The Road, Jack London, 1907

The main problem with hitchhiking is that it is considered illegal in the 50 states to hitchhike on the limited-access highways which are the best roads to hitchhike upon. Elsewhere in Connecticut it is legal, thanks to the former Gov. Ella Grasso, but this is the only state where it is legal to hithhike, as far as I know. The laws will change and it is best to inquire within each state as to the legality of hitchhiking on the local roads. *The Hitchhiker's Field Manual,* by Paul DiMaggio, copyright 1975, has a very comprehensive section on the various state laws concerning hitchhiking and is well worth looking into for information on the states that you are planning to pass through. Be aware that this information could be out of date. Many, if not all, of the intersections on the major highways will have signs telling you if hitchhiking and pedestrians are allowed or not. I have read and have been told that Colorado is the worst state to hitchhike in because the law enforcement officers there strictly enforce the law, but I do not have personal experience of this. How seriously the local law enforcement officers are taking their job of maintaining safety on the highways will be the main determining factor of how much of a bother it will be to hitchhike in any area. If there have been any recent crimes concerning hitchhikers, then the officers will be stricter than if there have been no recent problems. But since the officers have your safety and the safety of the drivers on that highway foremost in their minds, do not be offended by their actions toward you, for after all, it is for your own good. The survey of police officers in the Denver area done by the University of Colorado at Denver says that only 39.0% of the 113 officers surveyed feel that there is some danger involved in hitchhiking. These dangers come from crime, traffic hazards and traffic congestion. 22% of the

officers were impartial towards hitchhiking and 20.3% felt that it should
be allowed with restrictions such as designated spots from which to
hitchhike and registration of hitchhikers.

Coping with the police is simple if you follow one of the basic
tenets of all the world's religions; treat others as you would like them
to treat you. Be polite and courteous and don't start shouting about
your rights the moment the officer asks you to step over to the car.
The officer has probably had a worse day than you have had so don't
make it any harder on him or her. If you don't have any identification
papers on you, of course he or she will detain you just to make sure
that you are not an escaped felon or a runaway. If you don't have any
money on you, they may feel that you might be a burden to their
jurisdiction by being a vagrant and begging or stealing from someone.
This is the moment when that spare bit of money hidden away in your
pack will pacify their thoughts and allow you to continue onwards. Not
by trying to bribe them with it of course, but by showing that you have
enough money to reach your destination they will not treat you as a
vagrant. Common sense will tell you that carrying drugs, weapons, or
other such foolishness around with you is only increasing your chances
of being arrested and it is not worth it, no matter how good the drugs
are. Most of the time, the cops don't want to bother with hitchhikers.
Don't do anything that will force them to bother you.

You can greatly decrease your chances of having the police stop to
give you a little talk by staying out of their way. Stay off the pavement
of the highway. Always stand on the shoulder of the road, as this will
keep you out of the flow of traffic and lessen the chances of an officer
seeing you as a danger to drivers. If you do get dropped off at a spot
where you can't help but stand on the pavement, look around and see
if you can walk to a better spot. If an officer does stop, you can always
plead that your last ride dropped you off here and that you don't know
where a safer place is. If you stay on the entrance ramps, this will
please the police even more but it will cut down on the number of cars
that will see you hitchhiking.

A friend of mine told me the story of how he was hitchhiking in
Oklahoma back to his army base at Fort Sill and an Oklahoma state
trooper pulled over to talk to him. After giving him the usual talk of

how hitchhiking was illegal and dangerous, he gave him a ride down the road to the end of his jurisdiction and called ahead to another state trooper to pick him up. The second trooper also gave him a 25 mile ride and called ahead to a third, who also gave him another 25 mile ride to Fort Sill. So my friend rode 75 miles with 3 Oklahoma state troopers back to his base. I've heard of this sort of thing happening to enlisted men often enough to know that it is true, and I have gotten short rides with officers of the law, but don't plan your trip around this sort of luck.

Being stranded for a long time at an intersection is another one of the problems of hitchhiking, and you will just have to accept this as part of traveling via thumb. The time that you spend there is a very good time for thinking, and you will be amazed at the thoughts that will drift in, uncalled and unlooked for. You can meditate, sing, compose poetry, curse, or just scream, all excellent time wasters that I have used at one time or another. This is a good time to write down your experiences so far on the road and anything else that you want to remember.

If you notice that a driver is taking you out of your way, politely but firmly ask that you be let out. Explain that you know what you are doing and where you wish to go and that you know that this is the best way for you to travel in this area. However, being taken a little bit out of your way may sometimes work to your advantage. One such case was when a middle-aged man took me through Cheyenne, Wyoming on Route 30 instead of dropping me off on Route 80 as I wished. He said that he would drop me off right by Route 80 on the other side of Cheyenne. I just accepted it for the best and took a good look at the town of Cheyenne. Well, after walking 2 miles from where he let me off, I got back on Route 80, all the time cursing him for being an old fool for dropping me off where he did and cursing myself for being a young fool for accepting his ride through town. But the next driver that stopped for me took me all the way from Cheyenne to near Akron, Ohio. I might not have gotten that ride if I had gotten to the exit any sooner so there was both good and bad in the fact that I was taken slightly out of my way. You will notice that many of your rides work out this way.

I have already mentioned drunk and obnoxious drivers, and the best policy is to just not get into their vehicle if you smell alcohol as you open the door. Just ask where they are going and then say that you will try for a ride to a different destination, thank you. If they get insistent that you get in, tell them that it is your practice never to ride with anyone who has been drinking and walk away from the car towards the oncoming traffic.

It is a good idea to mention to every driver that you call back home every day to your parents and tell them where you are and where you are heading next. If the driver has any unfriendly ideas, this should help to curb them. And it is a good idea to contact your folks and tell them how you are doing since this will decrease their worries about you.

While I was sitting eating lunch at an entrance ramp in San Clemente, California, another hitchhiker came walking up. Since I was taking a short break from the heat of the day, I told him to go ahead and hitchhike. We talked of our travels, road courtesy, rides we get and the types of drivers that are likely to pick up hitchhikers. As we are talking, a pickup truck drives up the ramp and a young boy of about 7 or 8 leans out of the window and yells, "Get a haircut, freak". We both agreed that it was probably the father who was driving that told him to yell it and that was a bad way to prejudice the boy while he was young. This is one of the smaller hassles that you might come across while you are hitchhiking, abuse because of your physical appearance. I have had objects thrown at me while hitchhiking, usually empty beer bottles, but none ever came close enough to even make me move. Other hitchhikers have told me that this has happened to them also. Lots of people warned me about the "rednecks" in the south, but I never had any sort of problems while hitchhiking through the south and I met many fine, helpful people.

> "The cops would check you out, sure, but they always let you go. The ones in small towns even winked, wished you luck. And God bless the one in northern Idaho on a rainy spring an eternity ago who let me sleep in a dry jail cell."
>
> Steve Spence, *Car and Driver,*
> March 1991

SLEEPING ON THE ROAD

"When Richard Curtis roams from his native home in the Berkshires, he tends to sleep in the most outlandish places. He has curled up in his sleeping bag in the Parthenon; the Idaho pavilion at the 1974 World's Fair in Spokane, Wash.; a garden at Expo '67 in Montreal; a Little League announcer's box in Wyoming; and a Cleveland airport shower stall.

Plus: unlocked trailers, yachts, trucks and buses, buildings under construction and renovation, hotel conference rooms, graveyards and more prosaic bunks, fields and benches."

The Boston Globe, October 18, 1981.
Reprinted courtesy of The Boston Globe.

On any extended hitchhiking trip you can expect to spend several nights sleeping out wherever darkness or tiredness catches you so you should be prepared by bringing along the proper gear. The extra weight factors of carrying along a sleeping bag or blankets and a poncho or a ground cloth will mean nothing when you are caught out in the cold, rain or snow and you snuggle into your sleeping bag warm and dry. If you have not brought along this gear, or even if you have, the first thing to do is to get out of the wind and rain. If there are woods nearby, the trees will block some of the wind if you walk into the woods a ways and the rain or snow is less likely to fall on you if you cuddle as close as possible to a tree trunk. Evergreens are especially good for this and if you pile up the pine needles, it makes a soft spot to lie upon. At most highway intersections, there has been some landscaping done with trees and bushes and these can be used to block the weather.

I have very good memories of camping out in such varied spots as a park in Ashland, Montana, alongside the road near Greenwood, Mississippi in a thunderstorm, watching the sunset from a cornfield in Minnesota, seeing the sunrise from the Florida beach, and many others. Write down your experiences, good and bad, and take pictures with your camera in order to remember such times.

If you are near an overpass on the highway, walk underneath it and look up. You will see on most types a shelf up near the side of the overpass, directly underneath the overhead road surface. Admittedly the concrete is cold and hard to sleep on and it is smelly with exhaust fumes and noisy with the passing traffic, but at least it is a dry place to lie down. If you can find some cardboard or newspaper nearby, so much the better. Look for cardboard in the trash barrels or dumpsters at the restaurants or gas stations at that exit. Place some of it underneath you on the ground or concrete to slow the chill of the ground from soaking into you and place some of it over you to block out the wind and trap a bit of air around your body which will provide insulation. Also if you wish, you may crumple up some newspapers and place them inside your outer layer of clothes, and this old hobo's trick will provide another layer of air to trap more of your body's heat.

You might find an abandoned building nearby in which to spend the night. This will get you out of the weather but might also shelter other persons that you might not wish to meet. There may also be problems with being charged with trespassing if you are caught there by the owners or by the police. It will have to be a judgment call in each case if you should try it or not. Personally, I have never been bothered.

Since the weather factors will affect your traveling, you should have decided what to take along to be prepared for the worst weather that is possible at that time of year. Even though I started hitchhiking in August on one trip, I carried along a pair of long underwear, a wool hat and gloves, and a sweater that I could put on underneath my fatigue jacket because I knew that I would be passing through the northwest, where it does get chilly at night in late summer. My precautions were well founded and I used all of those items while in Montana and Idaho. If you have never traveled in the southwest, you will be surprised at how cold it can get at night after a scorchingly hot day. During the day you will wonder why you are carrying a sleeping bag in 100 degree heat, and at night you will be glad you did. If you are going to be out on the road during the winter, bring along the clothes you would wear if you were going to be working outside in the snow; items like long underwear, a wool hat, wool inner gloves and leather outer gloves, and many pairs of good socks. You lose a lot of body heat from your head, hands and feet so bring items to cover them. You might want to carry something to cover your face but don't wear it while hitchhiking. You want the drivers to see your smile.

When you are sleeping out while traveling, it is advisable to do so out of sight of the traffic on the road and of any pedestrians that may walk by. If you go into a wooded area to sleep, you can tie up your poncho or groundcloth to the trees using a length of nylon cord; this will provide you with a tent or a windbreak. In fields make sure that you do not lie down in a swampy or wet area which will make sleeping rather unpleasant. Sleeping underneath the bridges at overpasses is, as I have stated, noisy, smelly, and cold from the concrete, but it is a place to get away from the worst of the weather and the sight of all passersby. I am sure that most of the drivers going by will never have the faintest notion that off in that clump of trees by the exit or under the bridge that they just passed over, a person is catching his or her nightly rest.

As with any camping done out in the open, you will be bothered by some sort of pest, winged, crawling, two or four legged. Mosquitoes and other small biting creatures are pretty hard to defend yourself against unless you carry along insect repellent or sleep totally inside your sleeping bag. Most animals will just be curious as to what a human is doing sleeping out in their territory and won't bother you, aside from the initial fright when you wake up to discover a dog or cow standing over you. The human pests are the ones that you have to worry about and by placing yourself out of sight of the road, you will greatly reduce the possibility of someone bothering you. I have noticed that sleeping out in any exposed area has made me a very light sleeper, subject to awakening at any out of the ordinary noise, and I suspect this will also happen to you.

A good idea when you are sleeping out is to put your valuables into the bottom of your sleeping bag. No one will be able to get to them this way without waking you up. You can also use your knapsack for a pillow and prevent someone from making off with it. Also, if the weather is turning cold, you may want to put your clothes or boots into the bottom of your sleeping bag and this way they will be warm when you get up in the morning.

"Anyone who finds it difficult to sleep on the ground need only walk fast for two or three hours before lying down for the night and he will be astonished how quickly he falls asleep. There is something about sleeping on the earth which is more refreshing than sleeping in a bed, so that one awakens at sunrise filled with new life, although in the city it is often difficult to rise before ten o'clock."

"The Art of Hitch-Hiking"
Hugh Hardyman, *The New Republic,*
July 29, 1931

Some items I have read in the course of writing this book have recommended walking into the State and Federal parks across the nation in order to find a place to sleep. I have not done this only because usually I was never near one when it was time to camp out for the night. I see no reason why it would not be possible to do so, even if the park rangers or park police ask you to pay an entrance fee. If the ride you are with is going into the park, they will usually pay the entrance fee for the vehicle.

Sleeping in the car of the driver that picked you up is not polite to the driver and so I do not recommend it, but most will understand if you tell them that you have had a hard day and are going to take a short nap if it is all right with them. However, if you do sleep in the car, you may miss the turnoff or exit that you had wished to take so be sure to ask the driver to wake you before you get to that point. This is where the map or atlas that you are carrying will come in handy as you can estimate how far and how long it is to that exit and whether or not you have time for a nap.

If your ride offers accommodations for the night, use your intuition and feelings for human nature to decide if the driver is trustworthy. Make sure that you can easily get back to the road you are traveling on, either by walking or having the driver take you back in the morning. Offering to do some work to help pay for the accommodations is a polite and adult course of action that will be appreciated by the driver, although most of them will refuse to let you do it. I have done such things as washing dishes, doing household chores, and doing small repair jobs to repay, in a small way, the kindness shown to me.

I was outside Abilene, Texas when the dark blue Ranchero pulled over. Two guys were up front so I jumped in the back. About 10 minutes later, the driver knocks on the back window, points to the beer in his hand that he had just taken out of a cooler next to him and points at the cooler in back. I opened the cooler but it was empty so

I just shrugged my shoulders at him. He passed a Coors beer out of his window to me. I sat there, drinking beer in the sunshine, thinking that riding in the back of pickup trucks is one great way to see the country since you get a much more panoramic view of the landscape than from inside. We flew down the road, passing everything in sight and I wondered how fast we were going. I turned and looked at the speedometer. I could see all the markings up to 90 mph but I didn't see the indicator. "Well", I thought, "if we do crash, at least I'll go quickly and with a beer in my hands". About one-half hour later, we made a stop for gas and beer and introduced ourselves. Ken, the driver, and the other fellow worked for a construction company and were heading home to Fort Worth for the weekend. We continued on and after dropping off the other fellow, Ken invited me to stay for the weekend and see the Dallas and Fort Worth area. He loaned me the use of his apartment which was an old trolley car a family bought, moved to their backyard, and made into an apartment. I spent the weekend with Ken and his friends, driving around the area with Ken pointing out his stomping grounds, meeting his parents, stealing watermelons from a truck that was broken down by the side of the road ("they'll get sunburned if they sit out here too long"), going to a barbecue and a pool party, and generally having a fine time. I made sure that I contributed my share of expenses towards food and drinks. Such are the fun times that happen to you while hitchhiking.

Most of the drivers that have picked me up have seemed willing to share almost anything that they had, a human trait that I find quite surprising in this age of the "me-generation". I have slept in the front seat of pickups while the owner slept in the camper on the back (only because there was no room in the camper), sneaked into hotel rooms that the drivers had paid for, slept on people's living room couches, and have had more meals bought for me than I can remember. I repaid, in a small way, the ride from Billings, Montana to Boise, Idaho by helping the driver shovel horse and cow manure out of the barn on his newly purchased ranch. I did this for three days and considered it a small price to pay for the ride, a place to stay, very fine home-cooked meals made by his wife, rides around that part of Idaho near Eagle, and good conversation. If the driver is giving me a real long ride, I offer to chip in some money for gas, or at least buy one meal for him or her during the trip. Such small gestures go a long way in making a pleasant trip.

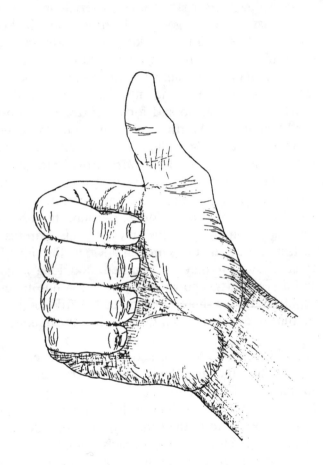

SEX ON THE ROAD

> " "So, you had sexual intercourse with the old man?" asked Dr. Robbins.
> "Repeatedly," blushed Sissy.
> "And how was it? I mean, how do you feel about it now?"
> "Er, I'm not really sure. You see, sex with Julian is like hitching a ride around the block on a fire engine. With the Chink, it was like hitching from Chicago to Salt Lake City in a big old nineteen fifty-nine Buick Roadmaster."
> "
>
> *Even Cowgirls Get The Blues,*
> Tom Robbins, 1976

I believe that perhaps 80% of the persons who pick up this book will turn to this chapter first to find out what titillating tales this author will tell. Were you one of them? If so, then you might be disappointed because I will offer no names or details of my experiences in this area. But don't worry, I'm working on an "X"-rated version of this book.

From my experiences, and from those of other hitchhikers that I know well enough to believe, I can say with a good degree of certainty that it does happen enough times to be a proven phenomenon but it is rare enough to be quite a pleasant surprise. In my many miles of traveling, I have been pleasantly surprised several times and I think I have been extremely lucky at that.

If you do get picked up by an individual of the opposite sex, don't assume that the driver picked you up just for the fun of having sex with you. There are many reasons why you may have been picked up and it would be foolish to assume that every driver of the opposite sex could not pass by that magnificent body of yours. If you do get picked up by a person of the opposite sex, do not blatantly inquire into whether they wish sexual favors from you. Doing this will most assuredly make the driver nervous and will probably result in that driver not picking up any more hitchhikers. Unless, of course, they want sexual fun and games and then it is a matter just between the two of you. However, with the prevalence of disease nowadays, I would most certainly take all the precautions that I could.

I have found that most women who picked me up were, after a

decent interval, quite comfortable discussing why they, a lone female, picked up a lone male. This has lead to quite interesting conversations about if they were ever worried about picking up hitchhikers or if they ever had problems with male hitchhikers who had assumed that the lady picked them up for sexual reasons only. Most of them assured me that they were good judges of character and rarely had problems. If a male hitchhiker did lead the conversation around to personal matters, the lady drivers said they either told him "no" outright or said that it was not a good time of the month for them. If a hitchhiker did get too fresh, pulling the car over to the side of the road and blasting the horn a few times to attract attention, and telling the hitchhiker to get out right then and there, handled all problems. Often I have been picked up by a car with two females in it and have been told that they felt safe enough being with the other to pick up hitchhikers but that they never pick anyone up when they were alone.

The few times that I ended up spending pleasant hours with the women who picked me up, all had one noticeable thing in common. They told me, a stranger passing through their lives, details of their lives and problems that I felt they were not sharing with their close friends. Perhaps this opportunity to unburden themselves, to discuss problems in their relationships, and know that it was not going to be talked about in their area or with their friends, was so needed by them, that they had to talk with someone. And who better than a stranger who would be gone that day or in the morning. In this manner, as a mostly passive listener to their problems, perhaps I sufficed as modifier or initiator for changes in their lives.

You might find that you are receiving sexual passes that you do not want. In my experience, the driver will lead the subject of conversation around to sex and then start quizzing you about your views and habits on the subject. This is not an area that I readily discuss with strangers and so I try to lead the conversation off in another direction or just do not answer any questions. If the driver does not take the hint and continues, I just tell them that I don't discuss my private life with strangers. Sometimes the driver at this point will become annoyed and continue quite graphically with the conversation or start reaching over in my direction. If this happens, I simply request to be let out of the vehicle and/or place their hand or arm quite roughly back away from me. They will get the idea and either let me out or change the subject. It is better to be standing in an unpleasant place than to be riding with an unpleasant ride. This is a problem that females hitchhiking by themselves will have more often than males will and so I recommend that they travel with another friend, either male or female. If one of you sits in the back seat, and one sits up front, the driver will usually be nervous enough wondering what the person in the back seat will do, that they will not try anything too forward.

You may also mention, if you have any uneasy feelings about the way the conversation or events are turning, that you are hitchhiking to wherever you are going because it has one of the best clinics for venereal diseases or AIDS research in that part of the country. This may cause the driver to become suddenly unfriendly or cause him to remember that he is taking the next exit but it is a good way of ensuring your safety.

KEEPING A JOURNAL WHILE ON THE ROAD

"My only ambition is to become a literary vagabond, with no possessions but a suitcase and a typewriter."
Reynolds Packard

"The whole object of travel is not to set foot on foreign land; it is at last to set foot on one's own country as foreign land."
G.K. Chesterton

I keep a journal while hitchhiking and I recommend that you do the same. It is quite interesting to look back several years later and remember what rides I received from where to where, who gave them to me and what these people were like at that time. I record daily events such as the weather, where I ate or slept, and any special events that happened such as meeting an army buddy's wife and newborn child, and meeting relatives that I knew about but had never met. You can write down ideas for projects, songs, or poetry that you come up with, or ideas for things that you wish to write about. You can write letters to people. You may wish to keep people's addresses that you meet or leave yours with them. I plan to mail copies of this book to many of the people who were nice enough to pick me up. I usually carry along a small pocket diary so that each day's events can be written down on that day's date and I also carry a small pad of paper to capture ideas, bits of poetry or songs (mostly bad) that I come up with, and any other thoughts that I wish to remember. The brain (well, at least my brain), for all of its marvels of memory storage and recall, has a lousy system for retrieving a specific bit of data at a specific time. Place the memory or thought down on paper, then if you lose the piece of paper you can say that at least you tried. A great deal of this book came from the bits and pieces of paper that I carried along with me.

I hitchhiked from upstate New York out to California to attend a friend's wedding in 1980. Here are the notes (edited) that I kept from that trip.

Monday, March 31, 1980 - start at 6:30 am.; -5 rides from NY to service plaza past exit 11 in Ohio; -guy in food service business to Wilkes-Barre;

-college guy to Bloomsburg; -Mass. guy in '70 bug to Lewisburg; -vet to exit 24; -stand in rain, sleet, snow for 2 1/2 hours (see section on The All Important Attitude); -Doug in '68 Ford pickup with camper to service area past exit 11 in Ohio. -rain, sleet, and snow all day; temperature in 30's & 40's.

Tuesday, April 1, 1980 - up at 6 am.; -12:30 reach Indiana; -past Chicago at 3:30 to 4; -camped 7:30 pm near Davenport, Iowa; -drove all day thru fog and some snow; temperature in 40's.

Wednesday, April 2, 1980 - up at 6 am. east Iowa; - 12:30 get to Omaha; -Doug drops me off at Grand Island; rain and snow; -2 drunk old boys in a pickup drinking whiskey and arguing if Jack Daniels or Southern Comfort was the better whiskey to Kearny; -get hitchhiking warning ticket (which I still have) from Trooper Rhodes, Badge 180 at mile marker 272; -Dan and Joy and their kids in a pink Rambler towing a U-haul take me to North Platte; -sneak into their hotel room to spend the night; cold and snowy.

Thursday, April 3, 1980 - drive with Dan all day; finally get to Little America, Wyoming at night; -sleep under highway bridge; -freeze; very cold with some snow.

Friday, April 4, 1980 - up at 5 am.; -George Shakespeare, an Arapaho, gives me a ride into Salt Lake City; -Scott gives me a ride into Reno, Nevada; -sleep under highway bridge again; -cold.

Saturday, April 5, 1980 - up at 6 am.; -2 rides over the Reno pass into Sacramento with Davis and Martinez; -many short rides into Hayward where I call Jerry; temperature in 60's in California; takes me all day to unthaw.

After spending the weekend with friends in the San Francisco area, I hitchhike to Los Angeles on Tuesday, April 9th. It takes me only 3 rides on route 5 because I have a sign that says "L.A.". I spend the week there and attend the wedding on April 12th wearing the suit that I had shipped out earlier via UPS. I ride back to the San Francisco area with friends and spend the next week playing tourist there before heading back east on April 21st.

Monday, April 21, 1980 - on road at 10 am.; -1st ride in a blue Datsun pickup gets into a minor accident; -6 rides to Sacramento; -stand for 3 hours, no rides; -eat in Eppie's 24 hour restaurant; -crash.

Tuesday, April 22, 1980 - up at 5:30 am., eat, on road at 6 am.; -1 ride to Auburn; -1 ride to Truckee in back of pickup truck with two young guys in rain and snow who give me Lowenbrau beer; -one ride over the pass into Reno; -eat at 76 Truck stop; -ride to Wadsworth with gambler; -ride to Toulow near Lovelock; -van to Beowawe with Mark, Judy, Fred, Dominick; -sleep off road in van; -cold.

Wednesday, April 23, 1980 - van folks give me ride to Wells; -from Wells, Nevada to Evanston, Wyoming with Ed Sullivan in Dodge Brougham motor home; -Ed is a realtor moving from California to Illinois who listens to motivation tapes while driving; -Champion Chemicals salesman gives me a ride to Little America and a Champion Chemicals baseball cap (which I still have); -sleep and freeze under the highway bridge again but no snow this time.

Thursday, April 24, 1980 - up at 5 am.; -breakfast; -1 ride to Rock Springs; -ride to just before Red Desert; -ride to Laramie; -old man to Cheyenne; -3:30 pm. Lance picks me up in a Datsun 280Z; -he is going to Ohio; -I drive across Nebraska as he naps; -he takes back over and drives thru the night.

Friday, April 25, 1980 - 7 am. we arrive in Illinois; -Lance drops me at exit 12 on Route 80 in Ohio at 5:30 pm.; -that one ride was 1306 miles; -1 ride with musician to exit 14; -1 ride to exit 15, 1 ride to exit 20 in Pennsylvania; -sleep under pine tree off of the exit; very cold but no snow.

Saturday, April 26, 1980 - up at 5 am.; -Tyler to Lock Haven exit & he buys me breakfast; -flight cap man to exit 27; -2 painters going to NYC drive me to route 81; -Dale to Scranton at noon; -West Virginia man into Binghamton area at 2 pm.

March 31st to April 6th: New York to California: 132 hours and 21 rides. Only hitchhiking during daylight.

April 21st to April 26th: California to New York: 124 hours and 28 rides. Only hitchhiking during daylight.

Why did I only hitchhike during the daylight hours? I was in no hurry and wanted to make sure that I would be seen by the drivers going past. Also note the fact that of the ten nights that I was spending out on the road, I received places to stay on four of them and one other was spent traveling through the night because the ride was traveling all night long.

> "I am constantly amazed at the dichotomy of prejudice and hate and friendliness that I run across - so many people have offered to help me, some for ulterior motives such as the trucker from Oxnard to L.A. who needed help to stay awake, some like Buz for no other reason than the goodness of his heart - I seem to have been used as a captive audience by some and as a sounding board by others, the only difference being the readiness and willingness of the person to modify their position in relation to new data they receive from me or others. Intelligence, I believe, is the main factor in determining the level of readiness to change; intelligence and a good sense of human character."

> Dale Carpenter, written in Thousand Oaks California. 1976

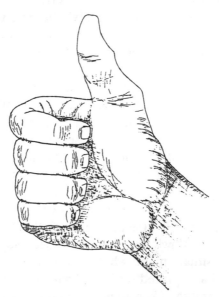

THE ALL IMPORTANT ATTITUDE

"Being on the road means learning to "be here now", taking each moment and extracting whatever it has to offer. You'll stand countless hours in dozens of places, struggling with the mysteries and miseries of reality. Gradually a feeling of contentment and fullness can be reached, no matter how forsaken and weird your situation may be. If it's a skill you want to acquire, then hitchhiking may be for you."

> From *Vagabonding in America: A Guidebook About Energy* by Ed Buryn and Stephanie Mines. Copyright 1973 by Ed Buryn. Reprinted by permission of Random House, Inc., and The Bookworks.

The most important thing that you need to take hitchhiking is the attitude that "YOU WILL GET A RIDE". If you stand there with the attitude or feeling that no one is going to pick you up and that you are wasting your time out there on the road, this attitude will be conveyed to the drivers of the vehicles through your body language and you won't get a ride. But if you stand there with the attitude of "YES, I'M GOING TO GET A RIDE AND IT WILL BE A GOOD RIDE AND IT WILL BE A LONG RIDE AND IT WILL BE A FAST RIDE", people will feel that and sense that and will be glad to pick you up. I believe that this attitude and a smile will reinforce each other and provide a stimulus that will attract drivers to you in some way.

I was hitchhiking in late March out to a friend's wedding in California and was dropped off at Exit 24 on Route 80 in western Pennsylvania on my first day of hitchhiking. I stood there for 2 hours and 30 minutes in rain, sleet, and light snow. It was cold enough to make it uncomfortable but not cold enough to make it really nasty. So for 2 hours and 30 minutes I cursed and stomped around and swore at the drivers, wishing all sorts of problems on them, and asking myself what in the name of the Wide Wide World of Sports I was doing out there (a question that I find myself asking every hitchhiking trip, usually on the first day). But slowly the attitude of acceptance asserted itself and I accepted my situation and what I was doing there. Shortly after that a ride stopped and picked me up. That one ride took me all the way to Omaha, Nebraska. Coincidence, you say? Not so, I reply. This occurrence has happened far too often for me to dismiss it as a lucky break in my favor.

A friend of mine with extensive hitchhiking experience calls this "Car-Karma", and explains it as "the longer the wait, the better the ride".

Once you have placed yourself into this "state of acceptance of the events that are about to happen to you", you will notice that a great deal of the worry and stress of travel will somehow no longer affect you. You might still wonder if the rides will carry you to a certain spot by a certain time but you will realize that you do not have a great deal of control over the events that will move you there, such as the number or the speed of the rides. The only control that you can bring to bear on this problem is the image that you project to the drivers that are going your way. And your projected state will be perceived as a person who is calm, aware, and yet eager and friendly for human contact and conversation. By maintaining this 'nomad' mentality and staying flexible, friendly, open-minded, and keeping a sense of wonder about what you are doing, you will ensure that your trip will be a success. Believe me, it gets results.

"There is something called the "rainstorm attitude". When caught in a sudden shower, one may determine not to get drenched, running as fast as one can or trying to thread one's way under the eaves of houses along the way - but one gets wet nonetheless. If from the outset one is mentally prepared to get wet, one is not in the least discomfited when it actually happens. Such an attitude is beneficial in all situations."

The Way of The Samurai,
Yukio Mishima, 1977,
Basic Books, Inc.

"Hitchhiking is about freedom, and a word you don't hear anymore: bliss. Sometimes I lie awake at night remembering the way the night sky looks in Arizona from the bed of a pickup. Once I saw Houston appear on the horizon at dawn out the window of a '53 Chevy with a southern sun coming up, a sun so big it gave me goosebumps. It was a sun I'd never seen before nor would again, it was a moment never to be repeated. Zen."

"Thumbs out." Steve Spence,
Car and Driver, March 1991

"But there are many for whom there is no satisfactory substitute for the crooked thumb, the pleading eye, the reluctant feet at the roadside. They take their chances with the policeman and they pick their "prospects" with a practiced eye. They set their sights on the far horizon and they keep going."

"Hitchhikers Ranks Grow Thin"
New York Times, July 25, 1937
Copyright 1937 by The New York Times
Company. Reprinted by permission.

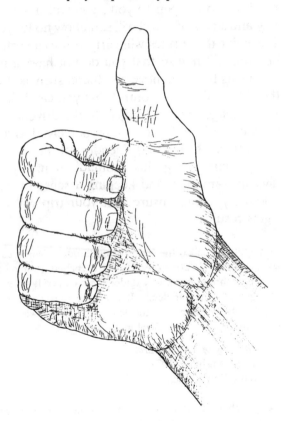

CONCLUSIONS AND RECOMMENDATIONS

Since the Colorado University study on hitchhiking is done so well and covers all of the points that I wish to discuss in this chapter on recommendations about hitchhiking, I will be quoting from it quite heavily.

" "Hitchhiking -- A Viable Addition to a Multimodal Transportation System?" is a study of the practice of Hitchhiking in the United States. It develops hard social, legal and planning data which dispels many of the myths that have developed and suggests some reforms that attack the real problems."

page i

"Today, hitchhiking is generally not well accepted, potentially dangerous, and illegal in many parts of the country; yet, many people rely on hitchhiking as a primary mode of transportation. The significance of hitchhiking lies in its potential as an alternative means of transportation. First, the United States is involved in an energy crisis, and a high percentage of available energy is required for transportation. It will be possible to avoid future energy crises only if alternative innovative approaches can be found to alleviate some of the country's pressing transportation problems. The problem of moving more people, goods, and services with more efficient use of energy can only be addressed if all available plans and proposals concerning various transportation techniques are adequately reviewed and tested. Mobility might be increased and total vehicle trips might be decreased through greater hitchhiking participation.

Second, as a "poor people's public transit," hitchhiking could expand the mobility potential of a segment of the population. There are some who simply cannot afford private transportation or even public transportation. These people are receiving differential treatment because of the financial realities of our society. An effort should be made to accommodate them and their needs."

page 1

An informal hitchhiking system has sprung up in Springfield, Virginia, according to an article in the *New York Times* dated October 1, 1984. Commuters meet in the parking lot of a restaurant that is easily accessible to one of the highways that flow into Washington, D.C. Drivers pull into the lot and state where they are going in the city. By

111

having enough passengers in a car, the drivers gain access to restricted commuter express lanes. Everyone shares expenses and gets to work faster. Perhaps this informal system could be tried in other areas.

> "Perhaps the safety factor afforded by hitchhiking laws could be preserved, while eliminating specific references to hitchhiking. A rule delineating unsafe pedestrian activities could serve this purpose and perhaps provide more protection of pedestrians than currently exists:
> "No person shall occupy space in that portion of the highway sustaining a regular flow of vehicular travel in a manner endangering himself or others or impeding traffic." "

page 71

> "There are four main grounds for challenging the constitutionality of laws restricting or prohibiting hitchhiking: vagueness, selective enforcement, punishment of status, and denial of freedom of movement."
> "Vagueness originates in unclear wording of the law, when reasonable men might differ in interpretation of its meaning."
> "The status of selective enforcement focuses in part on the vagueness of the law and, in part, on the class of individuals who commonly hitchhike: the young--often with long hair and without funds for other means of transportation. As is evident from the survey of law enforcement officials, different criteria are used to determine who is violating the hitchhiking statute, and variations were also apparent in enforcement practices."
> "Another contention tested in court is that antihitchhiking laws punish a status instead of an act; this argument, however, does not seem as strong as the other grounds for unconstitutionality. The law includes the phrase "for the purpose of soliciting a ride," which does not specify an act which is illegal. A person is thus punished for his purpose, not for a specific act. In other words, he is punished for holding the status of "hitchhiker" rather than for the actual act of hitchhiking."
> "The final argument is that restricting hitchhiking limits a person's freedom of mobility. Although this freedom is not specifically mentioned in either the United States or Colorado constitutions, it has generally been accepted in court. (Edwards V. California, 314 U.S. Court 160, 62 S. Ct. 164 (1941), et al.) Those who hitchhike because they lack access to other means of transportation are deprived of mobility by government prohibition of the practice."

pages 58, 59

> "The general public must provide either the impetus for a change in the law, or lend support to policy enacted by the legislature if change is to take place. The Federal Bureau of Investigation and other enforcement agencies have occasionally used terror tactic-type publicity to discourage hitchhiking,

but, despite these warnings, a majority of the public stated hitchhiking should be legal. According to the general questionnaire, a total of 69.1% said hitchhiking should be legal, including 54.22% who said hitchhiking should be limited by some type of regulation (e.g., designated hitchhiking spots or registration). This category was further broken down into those who felt hitchhiking should be legal even without restrictions, but would be improved by regulations, 39.2%; and those who said hitchhiking should be legal only with restrictions, 14.9%. Another 14.9% felt hitchhiking should be legal without any restriction. 22.7% were opposed to legalizing hitchhiking under any conditions.

The segment of the population who actually hitchhikes is generally without political power. As a group, they lack money for advertising and lobbying; many are too young to vote; they are a mobile segment of the population."

pages 62-63

"Aside from the strength of constitutional argument, there are several reasons that may account for judicial hitchhiking law. First, there has been no open public pressure to change the law, no political movement toward legalized hitchhiking. Second, hitchhiking, as a mode of transportation, has been hampered by its countercultural connotations from gaining widespread acceptance.

The final problem lies with the lack of organization on the part of hitchhikers themselves. According to ACLU President Peter Ney, there have been very few defendants willing to endure a long court battle over a petty offense with a fine of only $5 or $10, so few challenges have actually been made."

pages 63, 65

"In conclusion, legalized or controlled hitchhiking can be a beneficial addition to a community's transportation system. With public use and support, the system could supply a real need for a portion of the population, and could become a self-sufficient mode of transportation for the central city. Possible outcomes of this type of purposive intervention are many. Hitchhiking would be accessible to all, especially giving added mobility to low income people. An increase in traffic safety could be expected with a controlled system that employs designated areas for hitchhikers. Aside from having stops along highways and streets, gas stations, chain stores, restaurants, and parking lots could also be used.

Some level of registration that issues identification cards to hitchhikers and drivers would decrease the amount of crime involved. Ecologically, it would result in less gas consumption and less air pollution. It would also improve police-community relations, making the job of enforcement an easier one. This kind of transportation system where people depend on each other would generally promote a feeling of concern and cooperation in the community as a whole.

A legal system of hitchhiking, no matter what the final form, would be an effective addition to the maintenance of the central city, and the metropolitan area as a whole. If the quality of life is to be improved in and out of cities, more money, time, and energy must be channeled into systems that meet the needs of the people rather than alienating them."

page 111

I recommend a non-mandatory registration system for hitchhikers, done at the local or state level. This would be similar to the present automobile driver's license system. Fees charged, if any, must be kept low to encourage the lower economic strata to use the system. The fees should be used to set up designated hitchhiking spots within cities and along highways to provide safe spots from which to hitchhike. Hitchhikers, if registered, should display their registration cards when asked to by drivers or law enforcement officers. The main reason for my advocating this registration system is the increase in safety this will give the hitchhiker. Any hitchhiker may, if they choose, check in with the local office or chapter of the registration system. The hitchhiker could complain of problems with unfriendly or dangerous drivers, hazardous road conditions, or just check in to state that they were at that place at that time. The knowledge that a hitchhiker might have notified their parents and/or the authorities of their present location and future plans would make most drivers think more than twice about doing harm to any hitchhiker.

I foresee the possibility of businesses growing up to provide services to the hitchhikers, possibly like the Youth Hostels are now. Perhaps the friendly competition of time and distance hitchhiking, popular in the 1970's, would return. The 1979 *Guinness Book of World Records* mentions that in 1976, Raymond L. Anderson hitchhiked across all 48 continental United States in 14 days, 4 hours, 42 minutes and 5 seconds. Has anyone heard of a faster record? With the improvement of highways since then, I'm sure it could be beat, but we also have to factor in the current attitude against hitchhiking.

In conclusion, I believe that hitchhiking in the United States can be done safely; it can be enjoyable; it is about the best way to meet our citizens and see their lifestyles; and it will leave you with unique and unforgettable memories of the United States.

> "The only bad thing about hitchhiking is that it must end. And you must come to accept, like everyone else, the treadmill of living, the tediousness of routine. And what would you pay now for the bliss you felt on seeing the skyline of San Francisco for the very first time?"
>
> "Thumbs out." Steve Spence,
> *Car and Driver,* March 1991

Final Hints and Tips

Plan your trip. Decide what you want to do and see and choose the routes that will let you do this.

Dress for the weather.

Pack as little as possible.

Carry a sign. And a map.

Let friends and family know where and when you are going. This is for your safety and their piece of mind. Call them occasionally and let them know where you are and that you are safe and having fun.

Carry a camera and take plenty of pictures.

Wear good footgear. And bring a hat.

Stay as neat and clean as possible.

Carry identification.

Trust your intuitions.

On the highway of life, you do not want to end up wondering about roads not taken.

Always remember, you **will** get good rides. Sometimes it just takes longer then other times.

Smile.

About the author: Dale Carpenter has hitchhiked, so far, over 30,000 miles in the United States in all sorts of weather at all times of the year. Currently owning a car, he doesn't hitch as much as he used to. He rarely passes by a hitchhiker without giving them a lift.

If you wish to share your experiences hitchhiking or with hitchhikers, you may write to the author at the publisher's address. I am gathering material to use in another book on hitchhiking and in a future edition of this book. If I may use the material you send in, please indicate your permission to do so.

SELECTIVE BIBLIOGRAPHY

This bibliography represents the items that were available to the author, mainly East Coast newspapers and widely circulated magazines. The book would be much more representative of how hitchhiking is viewed nationwide if items from other areas of the country were accessible. Several of the books and movies mentioned were found by searching large libraries and film reference sources and may not be available in many areas. If an item was used or mentioned in the text, it is marked by a asterisk.

NEWSPAPERS

The Boston Globe

title	section, page & column	date
He's seen it all on his thumb and heart *	47	Oct 18, '81

New York Post

title	section, page & column	date
Deborah Harry's narrow escape	6	Nov 9, '89

New York Times

title	section, page & column	date
A new race of hobos takes the road * 4 8:1		Apr 11 '26
Hitchhikers end the season * 8 6:1		Sept 18 '27
Hitchhikers reveal odd lives and ways - feature article 10 14:1		Sept 30 '28
Mrs. F.D. Roosevelt gives lift to student 2:3		Sept 13 '35
Blind student hitches Calif. to NYC with dog 1:2		Aug 7 '36
3 sisters complete 3 month trip (AP) * 24:5		Aug 13 '36
79 year old returns to New Orleans from NYC after month on road 23:5		Sept 1 '36
Doctor reports headhunters have begun practice 2 2:7		July 11 '37
Hitchhikers ranks grow thin * 11 1:2		July 25 '37
Michigan to Panama and back 18:5		Aug 30 '38

117

Hitchhiking in England
10   9:4   July 23 '39
Gov. Ratner breaks own Kansas law against practice
                3:2   Jan 14 '40
Emily Post approves women defense workers hitching   *
                16:5   Dec 23 '42
Colorado Republican candidates plan hitchhiking campaigns
                17:6   Aug 28 '44
Australian airman hitches to Canada and back
  to Australia   4:5   Nov 14 '44
Mayor of Bowery crowns Miss Hitchhiker
                *   21:2   Aug 23 '46
Practice described in North China
                17:1   Sept 12 '48
H. Bennett hitches to Alaska & back to NYC in 17 days
                19:1   Aug 29 '51
Family of 5 goes from Toronto to NYC in 2 days
                25:6   July 23 '52
Max Fuks on world tour   5:3   Aug 3 '55
Couple (both in 40's) hike 14,000 miles in Canada and US
                27:4   Aug 9 '55
M. Lehmann, Swiss student, completes 19,000 mi.
  tour of US   *   17:4   Nov 10 '56
British youth tours US for 5 weeks
                17:5   Aug 24 '57
Auto Stop organizes hitching with coupon book & prizes
                4:2   Aug 2 '58
US hitcher visits 41 cities named after European cities -
  plans to visit European cities next
                79:3   Aug 16 '59
Organized hitching movement in USSR
                10:1   Apr 12 '64
5 Peace Corp girls hitch across Sahara
                1:6   Mar 3 '64
5 Peace Corp girls return - Monrovia to Liberia
                9:1   Mar 8 '64
Popularity and travails in Europe
                3:1   Aug 6 '67
Article by Hitchhiker's Handbook author - Tom Grimm
                10   1:1   Dec 13 '70
American Youth Hostel's advice
                10   1:1   Dec 13 '70
2 month trip on Inter-American Highway - north from Chile
                10   1:1   Dec 13 '70
Hitchhiking on "Autostop" in Europe
                10   1:5   Dec 13 '70
3 letters on Dec 13, 1970 articles on hitchhiking
                10   5:1   Jan 3 '71
Articles on hitchhiking across Canada
                10   10   June 20 '71
Thousands of youths hitchhiking this summer
                33:1   July 15 '71
Chicago Seed, underground paper, publishes
  hitching guide   33:1   Aug 8 '71
Hitchhiking jaunts on private airplanes
                10   1   Sept 19 '71

Canadian government encourages hitchhiking
                    10:4   June 26 '72
Man hitches 1,105 miles to vote - Wyoming to
  Rochester, Minn.   31:6   Nov 8 '72
NY Times survey finds increase in women hitchhiking
             *   1:5   Dec 26 '72
Engineer hitches to work, NJ to Manhattan, for 2 years
                    73:1   May 13 '73
Article on hitchhiking in Conn. after repeal of laws
                    33:3   June 9 '75
Various state laws on hitchhiking
             10   5   June 22 '75
New Jersey 4th of July hitchhiking increase expected
                    50:1   July 4 '75
NY Times survey - hitchhiker more likely to be victim
                    13:1   Oct 6 '75
Elderly woman hitchhiker in Scotland
             10   9   Jan 25 '76
Article on hitchhiking across England
             10   1   July 10 '77
Experimental program in Novato, CA
                    18:4   May 6 '79
Article urges motorists to give rides
                    23:1   Oct 9 '79
Advice to women hitchhikers
             *   11   27:1   Feb 24 '80
Ease of travel to NYC 2   3:3 Apr 3 '80
The new hitchhiking: white collars and trust
                    8:4   Oct 1 '84
3 Argentines hitch 27,00 miles
             1   6:6   Sept 20 '86
Ride wanted: purple cow going west
             1   16:1   July 16 '87
Hitchhiking organized in Wash., DC
             1   52:1   Feb 7 '88
Hitchhiking appears to be in decline
             *   1   18:1   Apr 3 '88
Wine: A choice encounter   Sept 4 '88
Thumbs up for new way to travel
                    12:1   July 9 '91

Washington Post
  title   section, page & column   date

Popularity in America increases - Travelers Aid
  Association study * L   10:1   Feb 20 '72
Traveling by thumb grows in popularity
             * C   1:1   Apr 10 '72
Hitchhiking across the Sahara discussed
                L   1:1   June 17 '73
Freight train hopping discussed
                L   1:1   Aug 15 '76
Column on California court ruling on alleged rape of
  hitcher *   A   23:1   July 27 '77
78th Annual Hobo's Convention - Britt, Iowa
                B   1:5   Aug 7 '78

```
King of Hobo's interviewed - Gordon (Bud) Filer
                    D      14:2                Sept 29 '78
Hitchhiker David Buckley discussed - 40,000 mile trip
  thru  North America   F      19:1           Oct 22 '78
```

MAGAZINES

title/mag	volume/starting page	date
Art of hitchhiking - New Republic		
*	67:283	July 29 '31
In the driftway - Nation		
*	135:233	Sept 14 '32
Thumb fun - Review of Reviews		
*	5:55	April '37
I pick 'em up - Scribner's Mag.		
*	105:2	Feb '39
Thumbs Across the Continent - Coronet		
*	10:1	May '41
Hitchhiking technique - Life		
	25:175	Sept 13 '48
Our footloose correspondents - New Yorker		
	24:68	Oct 2 '48
We saw America on $20.00 - Saturday Evening Post		
	222:26	Mar 11 '50
Hitchhiking with the yellow fish - Harper's Magazine		
	200:69	March '50
Driver's downfall - Newsweek		
	42:86	Sept 14 '53
Magnificent hobo - Holiday		
*	18:178	Dec '55
Hitchhiking in Europe - Atlantic		
	196:108	Dec '55
Diary of hitchhike across Sahara - Life		
	56:92	Apr 17 '64
Le stop - hitchhiking on the Continent - Time		
	83:61	May 15 '64
Rule of thumb for open road - Sports Illustrated *		
	24:76	June 6 '66
Cars & the law - Motor Trend		
	18:12	Dec '66
New rule of thumb - Newsweek		
	73:63	June 16 '69
Hitchhiking by air - Time		
	98:49	Aug 16 '71
Ride across America - Life		
	71:36	Aug 27 '71
Meditations on hitchhiking ticket - National Review		
	23:1069	Sept 24 '71
Thumbtripping by air - Esquire		
	76:56	Nov '71
Hitching nowhere - Harper's Magazine		
	245:66	Sept '72

An experimental investigation of hitch-hitching -
  Journal of Psychology   82:43   Sept '72
Rules of thumb - Newsweek   *
                             81:38   Feb 19 '73
Deadly new odds - Good Housekeeping
                             177:38   July '73
Rules of thumbing - Science Digest
                             75:70   Jan '74
What you should know before hitchhiking - Seventeen
                             33:58   Feb '74
Staring and compliance: A field experiment on hitchhiking
  - Journal of Applied Social Psychology
                             4:165   Apr '74
Rules of thumb - Sat. Review World
                             1:33   May 4 '74
Hitchhiking - PTA Magazine
                             69:30   Sept '74
On the road - Harper's Magazine   *
                             249:119   Nov '74
Good old with nothing - Esquire
                             83:78   April '75
Hitchhiking: Social signals at a distance - Bulletin of
  the Psychonomic Society   5:459   June '75
The sexually assaulted female: Innocent victim or
  temptress? - Canada's Mental Health
                             25:26   March '77
Writer on the road - Writer's Digest
                             57:20   April '77
Bullshitting: Road lore among hitchhikers -
  Social Problems   25:241   Feb '78
Predicting motorists' altruism - Psychological Reports
                             43:567   Oct '78
Thumbs up for commuters - McCalls
                             107:65   Nov '79
Notes & comments - New Yorker
                             56:29   Apr 21 '80
Along the highway... - Christian Science Monitor
                             72:20   Nov 17 '80
Sore thumbs. - Progressive
                             46:34   Aug '82
A hitchhiker's guide to Central America -
  Harper's Magazine   269:16   July '84
On the road again - Modern Maturity
                             :74   Jun/Jul '85
Personality characteristics of the crosscountry hitchhiker
  - Adolescence   20:655   Fall '85
Covering games, with a hitch - Sports Illustrated
                             :5   Mar 5 '90
The rise of the interstates - American Heritage of
  Invention & Technology   7:8   Fall '91
Thumbs out - Car and Driver   *
                             36:160   Mar '91
On a wing and a thumb - Video
                             15:7   Oct '91
When Big Bill France moved on Motown - Car and Driver
                             37:119   Oct '91

Perot on Perot - <u>U.S. News & World Report</u>
                        112:24   June 29 '92

BOOKS

Adams, Douglas. *The Hitchhiker's Guide to the Universe.* New York: Harmony Books. 1979. *
Allsop, Kenneth. *Hard Traveling.* New York: New American Library. 1967.
Anderson, Nels. *The American Hobo.* Leiden: E. J. Brill. 1975.
   Men on the Move. Chicago: University of Chicago Press. 1940.
   The Milk and Honey Route: A Handbook for Hobos. New York: Vangard. 1931.
Beck, Frank O. *Hobomania.* Rindge, New Hampshire: R. R. Smith. 1956.
Berg, Rick. *The Art and Adventure of Traveling Cheaply.* New York: The New American Library. 1979. *
Biering-Sorenson, Fin & Jorgensen, Torben. *Africa for the Hitchhiker.* Copenhagen: Bramsen & Hjort. 1976.
Brunvand, Jan Harold. *The Vanishing Hitchhiker; American Urban Legends and Their Meanings.* New York: W. W. Norton. 1981. *
   The Choking Doberman and Other "New" Urban Legends. New York: W. W. Norton. 1984.
   The Mexican Pet; More "New" Urban Legends and Some Old Favorites. New York: W. W. Norton. 1986.
Burns, Roger. *Knights of the Road: A Hobo History.* New York: Methuen. 1980.
Buryn, Ed and Stephanie Mines. *Vagabonding in America.* New York: Random House and Berkeley, California: The Bookworks; co-publishers. 1973. *
Childress, David Hatcher. *A Hitchhiker's Guide to Africa and Arabia.* Chicago: Chicago Review Press. 1984.
Coopersmith, Paul. *Rule of Thumb; A Hitchhiker's Handbook to Europe, North Africa, and the East.* New York: Simon and Schuster. 1973. *
Dahlberg, Edwin T. *I Pick Up Hitchhikers.* Valley Forge, Pennsylvania: Judson Press. 1978. *
Dallmeyer, Kenneth E. *Hitchhiking -- A Viable Addition to a Multimodel Transportation System?.* Colorado University, Denver. Sponsored

by National Science Foundation, Washington, D.C. Report Number: NSF/SOS-GY-11486. March 1975. *

Davies, William Henry. *The Adventures of Johnny Walker, Tramp.* London: Howard Baker. 1970.

The Autobiography of a Super-Tramp. London: A. C. Fitfield. 1908.

DeTitta, Tom. *I Think I'll Drop You Off in Deadwood: A Hitchhiker's Story.* Marietta, Georgia: Cherokee Publishing Company. 1989.

DiMaggio, Paul. *The Hitchhiker's Field Manual.* New York: Macmillan. 1973.

Douglas, William O. *Go East, Young Man.* New York: Dell Publishing Company. 1974.

Fletcher, Colin. *The Complete Walker; The Joys and Techniques of Hiking and Backpacking.* New York: Knopf. 1969.

Gay, Delph. *Beyond the Bus-stop; A Hitchhiker's Story.* Christchurch, New Zealand: Caxton Press. 1980.

Goss, Michael. *The Evidence for Phantom Hitch-hikers.* Wellingborough, Northamptonshire: Aquarian Press. 1984.

Grimm, Tom. *Hitchhiker's Handbook; A Most Unusual Guide to Hitchhiking in the United States.* Laguna Beach, California: Vagabond Press. 1970. *

Guthrie, Woody. *Bound for Glory.* New York: Doubleday. 1943.

Hawthorn, Margaret. *The American Youth Hostels' Bike/Hike Book.* New York: Stackpole Books. 1976.

Hicks, Ken. *The Complete Hitch Hiker.* New Canaan, Connecticut: Tobey Publishing Company. 1973.

Kennedy, Jeff & Greenberg, David E. *The Hitchhiker's Road Book; A Guide to Traveling by Thumb in Europe.* Garden City, New York: Doubleday. 1972.

Kerouac, Jack. *On the Road.* New York: Viking Press. Penguin Books USA Inc. 1955. *

Knies, Donald. *Walk the Wide World.* New York: Dodd, Mead & Company. 1958. *

Kuralt, Charles. *Dateline America.* New York: Harcourt Brace Jovanovich. 1979.

On The Road With Charles Kuralt. New York: G. P. Putnam's Sons. 1985.

Least Heat Moon, William. *Blue Highways; A Journey Into America.* New York: Ballantine Books. 1982. *

Livingston, Leon Ray. *The Curse of Tramp Life.* Erie, Pennsylvania: A-No 1 Publishing Company. 1912.
From Coast to Coast with Jack London. Black Letter Press. 1969.
Here and There with A-No 1. Erie, Pennsylvania: A-No 1 Publishing Company. 1921.
The Snare of the Road. Erie, Pennsylvania: A-No 1 Publishing Company. 1916.
Lobo, Ben & Links, Sara. *Side of the Road; A Hitchhiker's Guide to the United States.* New York: Simon and Schuster. 1972.
London, Jack. *The Road.* New York: Macmillan Company. 1907. *
Mathers, Michael. *Riding the Rails.* Boston: Houghton Mifflin. 1973.
Michener, James A. *The Drifters.* New York: Random House. 1971.
*
The World is My Home: A Memoir. New York: Random House. 1992.
Minehan, Thomas. *Boy and Girl Tramps of America.* New York: Farrar & Rinehart. 1934.
Lonesome Road, The Way of Life of a Hobo. Evanston, Illinois: Row, Peterson & Company. 1941.
Mishima, Yukio. *The Way of The Samurai.* New York: Basic Books, Inc. 1977. *
Newman, Steve M. *Worldwalk.* New York: William Morrow & Company. 1989. *
Robbins, Tom. *Even Cowgirls Get The Blues.* Boston: Houghton Mifflin. 1976. *
Seeger, Pete. *The Incompleat Folksinger.* New York: Simon & Schuster. 1972.
Sheehy, Gail. *Passages; Predictable Crises of Adult Life.* New York: E. P. Dutton. 1974.
Steinbeck, John. *Travels With Charley: In Search of America.* New York: Viking Press. 1962.
Terkel, Studs. *Hard Times: An Oral History of the Depression.* New York: Avon. 1971.
Tully, Jim. *Beggars of Life.* New York: Garden City Publishing Company. 1924.
Wachsberger, Ken. *Beercans on the Side of the Road: The Story of Henry the Hitchhiker.* Ann Arbor, Mich.: Azenphony Press. 1988.
Welsh, Ken. *Hitchhiker' Guide to Europe; the 1986 Guidebook for*

People on a Hitchhiking Budget. New York: Grove Press. 1986.

Weiss, Walter F. *America's Wandering Youth; A Sociological Study of Young Hitchhikers in the United States.* Jericho, New York: Exposition Press. 1974.

Wernig, Phil. *The Hitchhikers.* Milbrae, California: Celestial Arts Publishing. 1972.

Willard, Josiah Flynt. *My Life.* New York: Outing Publishing Company. 1908.

Tramping with Tramps. Montclair, New Jersey: Patterson Smith Publishing Company. 1972.

Wurster, John Andersen, editor. *Let's Go; The Student Guide To America; 1969.* Cambridge, Mass.: Harvard Student Agencies. 1968.

MOVIES

Anything Can Happen; Tout Peut Arriver. 1969. 80 minutes. France. Director: Philippe Labro. Jean-Claude Bouillon, Prudence Harrington, Fabrice Lucchini. A journalist hitchhikes around France searching for his former wife.

Atlantic City. 1980. 104 minutes. Canadian-French. Director: Louis Malle. Burt Lancaster, Susan Sarandon, Kate Reid, Michel Piccoli, Hollis McLaren, Robert Joy. A small-time crook gets a aging hood involved in heroin dealing in Atlantic City. Worth seeing for the scenes of the crook hitchhiking with too much luggage, heroin, and a pregnant woman and the scenes of The Burns Sisters.

Con-Fusion; Con Fusion. 1980. 100 minutes. Italy. Director: Piero Natoli. Carlotta Natoli, Piero Natoli, Luisa Maneri. A look at the relationship between a man, his daughter, and a hitchhiker the man befriends.

Creepshow 2. 1987. 89 minutes. USA. Director: Michael Gornick. Three episodes make up this film based on stories written by Stephen King. In one of them, a woman is haunted by the hitchhiker that she ran over.

Cross Country Romance. 1940. 67 minutes. USA. Director: Frank Woodruff. Gene Raymond, Wendy Barrie, Hedda Hopper, Billy Gilbert, George P. Huntley, Berton Churchhill. A girl hitchhikes across the country with a doctor and falls in love with him.

Detour. 1946. 69 minutes. USA. Director: Edgar G. Ulmer. Tom Neal, Claudia Drake, Ann Savage, Edmund MacDonald, Tom Ryan. After the driver of the car that picks him up dies of a heart attack, a hitchhiker takes the man's car and wallet. He picks up a female hitchhiker who accuses him of murdering the driver and bullies him into swindling money from a wealthy man. Intriguing film.

The Devil Thumbs a Ride. 1947. 63 minutes. USA. Director: Felix Feist. Lawrence Tierney, Ted North, Nan Leslie, Betty Lawford,

Andrew Tombes, Harry Shannon. A young salesman driving from San Diego to Los Angeles picks up a male hitchhiker and then two women hitchhikers. It turns out that the male hitchhiker has just killed a man.

Diary of a Teenage Hitchhiker. 1979. 100 minutes. USA. Director: Ted Post. Dick Van Patten, Katherine Helmond, James Carroll Jordan, Charlene Tilton, Katy Kurtzman. This made for television movie covers the usual ground about a teenage girl who doesn't listen to her parent's advice about accepting rides from strangers.

Dolls. 1987. 77 minutes. USA. Director: Stuart Gordon. Ian Patrick Williams, Carolyn Purdy-Gordon, Carrie Lorraine, Guy Rolfe, Hilary Mason. A storm forces a family, a businessman, and two hitchhikers to take shelter at a dollmaker's house. The dolls come alive and punish the evildoers in the group.

The Drifter. 1988. 88 minutes. USA. Director: Larry Brand. Tim Delaney, Timothy Bottoms, Al Shannon, Miles O'Keefe, Anna Gray Garduno. A fashion designer has a short affair with a hitchhiker who helps her change a flat tire. When she wishes to end the relationship, he becomes violent.

The Electric Horseman. 1979. 120 minutes. USA. Director: Sydney Pollack. Robert Redford, Jane Fonda, Valerie Perrine, Willie Nelson, John Saxon, Nicolas Coster. Robert Redford is a has-been rodeo rider who steals a $12 million thoroughbred being used in Las Vegas to advertise the products of the corporation who owns the horse and sets out to turn the horse free to roam the range with wild mustangs. Hitchhiking scene is incidental but it ties in beautifully with the sense of freedom and adventure people associate with hitchhikers.

Field of Dreams. 1989. 106 minutes. USA. Director: Paul Alden Robinson. Kevin Costner, Amy Madigan, Gary Hoffman, Ray Liotta, Timothy Busfield, James Earl Jones, Burt Lancaster. A farmer is inspired by a ethereal voice to build a baseball diamond in his cornfield. This brings about the return of baseball legend "Shoeless" Joe Jackson and other baseball greats. While on a quest across the country to explain this happening, the farmer picks up a hitchhiker because, as he explains, "I can use all the good karma I can get". A must-see film.

Foul Play. 1978. 115 minutes. USA. Director: Colin Higgins. Goldie Hawn, Chevy Chase, Burgess Meredith, Rachel Roberts, Dudley Moore, Brian Dennehy, Marc Lawrence, Billy Barty, William Frankfather. A librarian picks up a hitchhiker who is an undercover cop pursued by a gang of assassins. He leaves a roll of microfilm with her (without her knowledge) and then is murdered. The gang then pursues her. Good fun. Comedy/romance/suspense.

The Gumball Rally. 1976. 107 minutes. USA. Director: Chuck Bail. Michael Sarazin, Tim McIntire, Raul Julia, Susan Flannery, Gary Busey, Steven Keats, J. Pat O'Malley. Cross-country road race from New York City to Long Beach includes lots of action, wrecks, and fine cars. Hitchhiking plays a small but pivotal part. Comedy/action.

Heroes Are Not Wet Behind the Ears; Les Heroes N'Ont Pas Froid Aux Oreilles. 1978. 83 minutes. France. Director: Charles Nemes. Daniel Auteuil, Gerard Jugnot, Anne Jousset, Patricia Karim, Henri Guybet. Two provincial cousins who work in a bank manage to get a vacation and find adventures which include meeting a female hitchhiker.

High Rolling. 1977. 89 minutes. Australia. Director: Tgor Auzins. Joseph Bottoms, Grigor Taylor, Judy Davis, John Clayton, Wendy Hughes. Two carnival workers decide to hitchhike around the country. When one of them is attacked by a homosexual drug pusher, they steal the pusher's car and wallet. The drug pusher gives chase.

The Hitcher. 1986. 97 minutes. USA. Director: Robert Harmon. Rutger Hauer, C. Thomas Howell, Jennifer Jason Leigh, Jeffrey DeMunn. A teenager picks up a hitchhiker in the Southwest. The hitchhiker tells the teenager that he has been murdering people that pick him up and that now he plans to do the same to the teenager. Thus starts a long, gory chase between the two. This is the sort of film that gives a bad image to hitchhikers. Frightening.

Hitchhike!. 1974. 78 minutes. USA. Director: Gordon Hessler. Cloris Leachman, Michael Brandon, Henry Darrow, Cameron Mitchell, John Elerick, Linden Chiles. A made-for-television movie about a lonely middle-aged women who picks up a hitchhiker who has just killed his stepmother. Haven't we seen this sort of story before?

The Hitchhikers. 1972. 91 minutes. USA. Director: Fred Sebastian and Beverly Sebastian. Misty Rowe, Norman Klar, Linda Avery, Tammy Gibbs, Kathy Stutsman, Mary Thatcher. A band of marauding hippies use women hitchhikers to lure men whom they then rob. Another sex film which gives hitchhikers a poor image.

It Happened One Night. 1934. 105 minutes. USA. Director: Frank Capra. Clark Gable, Claudette Colbert, Walter Connolly, Roscoe Karns, Alan Hale. Heiress runs away from her wedding and meets reporter, who helps her first to gain a story, and then out of love. She shows him how to hitchhike. A must-see film. This film won four Academy Awards for Best Picture, Director, Best Actor and Best Actress.

It's a Mad Mad Mad Mad World. 1963. 192 minutes. USA. Director: Stanley Kramer. Spencer Tracy, Edie Adams, Milton Berle, Sid Caesar, Buddy Hackett, Ethel Merman, Mickey Ronney, Dick Shawn, Phil Silvers, Jonathan Winters, and many guest stars. A group of people come upon a recently relased convict dying from a car accident, who tells them he buried a great deal of money "under a big W". They race to find it, by any means possible, all the while being tracked by a police detective. Chases, crashes, spills, jokes, slapstick galore.

Juke Girl. 1942. 90 minutes. USA. Director: Curtis Bernhardt. Ann Sheridan, Ronald Reagan, Richard Whorf, Gene Lockhart, Betty Brewer, Faye Emerson, Alan Hale, Howard de Silva. Two hitchhikers traveling through Florida get involved in a feud between farmers and packers, a shop girl, and a murder.

Knife in the Water; Noz W Wodzie. 1962. 94 minutes. Poland. Director: Roman Polanski. Leon Niemczyk, Jolanta Umecka, Zygmunt Malanowicz. Roman Polanski's first film is a drama focusing on the tensions that result when a middle-aged couple pick up a young hitchhiker and invite him to go sailing with them for the weekend. A fine film.

L.A. Plays Itself. 1972. 55 minutes. USA. Director: Fred Halsted. Fred Halsted, Joey Yanichek, Jim Frost, Rick Coates. A truck driver picks up hitchhikers and subjects them to various sexual perversions. Another film which makes it difficult for us hitchhikers.

Leaving Normal. 1992. 109 minutes. USA. Director: Edward Zwick. Meg Tilly, Christine Lahti, Patrika Darbo, Lenny Von Dohlen, James Gammon. A worldly cocktail waitress rescues a vulnerable, optimistic woman running away from her husband and gives her a ride first to Portland, and then on to Alaska. After their car is vandalized, they take to the road and find out that sometimes leaving everything to fate is better then making choices. "Sometimes the only way to find where you are going is to lose your way." Quite interesting.

Many Passed By; Viele Kamen Vorbei. 1956. 85 minutes. Germany. Director: Peter Pewas. Harald Maresch, Francis Martin, Christian Doermer, Heinz Schimmelpfenning, Hans-Hermann Schaufuss. A semi-documentary film about a psychopath who picks up young women hitchhikers and strangles them. Based on true events.

Mean Dog Blues. 1978. 108 minutes. USA. Director: Mel Stuart. Gregg Henry, George Kennedy, Kay Lenz, Scatman Crothers, Tina Louise, Felton Perry, James Wainwright. A hitchhiker is falsely accused of a death and sent to a prison work farm run by sadistic overseers and guarded by Dobermans. Action film.

The Milky Way; La Voie Lactee. 1969. 102 minutes. France and Italy. Director: Luis Bunuel. Paul Frankeur, Laurent Terzieff, Alain Cunt, Edity Scob, Bernard Verley, Jean-Claude Carriere. Two French tramps make a pilgrimage to the tomb of the Apostle James in Spain, encountering many of the individuals and symbols from the Christian religion along the way. Haunting, funny, thoughtful film. A must-see.

The Night Holds Terror. 1955. 85 minutes. USA. Director: Andrew Stone. Jack Kelly, Hildy Parks, Vince Edwards, John Cassavetes, David Cross, Edward Marr. A man gives a hitchhiker a ride, only to have the hitchhiker and two friends move into his house and terrorize him and his family while holding them for ransom.

The Rain People. 1969. 101 minutes. USA. Director: Francis Ford Coppola. James Caan, Shirley Knight, Robert Duvall, Tom Aldredge, Robert Modica, Marya Zimmet. A woman leaves her home and husband on a journey of self-discovery. She picks up a hitchhiker who she discovers is mentally crippled and then can't get rid of him. This leads into a meeting and a relationship with a motorcycle cop. Drama.

Return to Macon County. 1975. 90 minutes. USA. Director: Richard Compton. Don Johnson, Nick Nolte, Robin Mattson, Robert Viharo, Eugene Daniels, Matt Greene. Youngsters get mixed up with drag races, sex, the law, violence and murder. And some hitchhiking.

Road Games. 1981. 100 minutes. Australia. Director: Richard Franklin. Stacy Keach, Jamie Lee Curtis, Marion Edwards, Grant Page, Bill Stacey. A truckdriver pursues a killer and picks up a hitchhiker on the way. Thriller.

Roadhouse 66. 1984. USA. Director: John Mark Robinson. William Defoe, Judge Reinhold, Kaaren Lee, Kate Vernon, Stephen Elliot, Alan Autry. A East Coast Ivy Leaguer meets a hitchhiker, get the local toughs mad at them, meet two pretty girls, get involved with a local road race, and face their personal problems over the Labor Day weekend in a small Arizona town. Worth a look.

Sammy Going South; A Boy Ten Feet Tall. 1963. 128 minutes. Great Britain. Director: Alexander MacKendrick. Edward G. Robinson, Fergus McCelland, Constance Cummings, Harry H. Corbett, Paul Stassino. An orphaned boy travels south alone through Africa from Port Said to his aunt in Durban.

Something to Hide. 1972. 100 minutes. Great Britain. Director: Alastair Reid. Peter Finch, Shelly Winters, Colin Blakely, John Stride, Linda Hayden, Harold Goldblatt. After picking up a hitchhiker who is in an advanced state of pregnancy and taking her to his house, a man can not get rid of her.

Stopar; The Hitchhiker. 1979. 90 minutes. Czechoslovakia. Director: Peter Tucek. Josef Vinklar, Ivanka Devata, Julie Juristava, Oldrich Navratil. A husband and his mistress pick up a hitchhiker on their way to a weekend rendezvous. The car breaks down, the hitchhiker is repairing it, and the man's wife and daughter drive by.

Thelma & Louise. 1991. USA. Director: Ridley Scott. Susan Sarandon, Geena Davis, Harvey Keitel, Michael Madsen, Christopher McDonald, Brad Pitt. Two women start out for a long weekend at a friend's vacation retreat but protecting one of them from a rape attempt by killing the rapist throws them into flight from the law. A hitchhiker who they pick up admits to robbing stores for a living ands teaches them the tricks of his trade. A must see film.

The Thin Blue Line. 1988. 106 minutes. USA. Director: Errol Morris. David Harris, Errol Morris, Randall Adams. A docudrama about the shooting of a Dallas police officer who was shot after pulling over an automobile. The driver of the car blamed the shooting on the hitchhiker he had picked up. Based on true events.

3 Into 2 Won't Go. 1969. 93 minutes. Great Britain. Director: Peter Hall. Rod Steiger, Claire Bloom, Judy Geeson, Peggy Ashcroft, Paul Rogers, Lynn Farleigh. The story of a love triangle between a career-oriented businessman, his wife, and the free-spirited young hitchhiker that he meets while on a business trip.

Thumb Tripping. 1972. 94 minutes. USA. Director: Quentin Masters. Michael Burns, Meg Foster, Marianna Hill, Bruce Dern, Mike Conrad, Joyce Van Patten. Two hitchhikers meet and agree to travel together and share their experiences.

Truck It. 1973. 44 minutes. USA. Director: Fred Halsted. A farce about a naked man who drives a van, picks up hitchhikers and lets them do whatever they want in the back of the van. Sure, happens all the time all over the country.

Two For The Road. 1967. 112 minutes. Great Britain. Director: Stanley Donen. Albert Finney, Audrey Hepburn, Williams Daniels, Eleanor Brown, Claude Dauphin, Jacqueline Bisset. A couple meet and fall in love while hitchhiking through France and, twelve years later, look back upon their marriage and their efforts to save it. Drama. A beautiful film.

Two-Lane Blacktop. 1971. 102 minutes. USA. Director: Monte Hellman. James Taylor, Warren Oates, Laurie Bird, Dennis Wilson, David Drake, Harry Dean Stanton. The film focuses on the interactions of four rootless characters who meet while traveling across the country. Low key but intense. Worth watching.

Wild Strawberries. 1957. 90 minutes. Sweden. Director: Ingmar Bergman. Victor Sjostrom, Bibi Anderson, Injrid Thulin, Gunnar Bjornstrand, Jullan Kindahl, Naima Wifstrand. While traveling with his daughter-in-law to an awards ceremony, an old man picks up three hitchhikers.

The Wizard of Oz. 1939. 101 minutes. USA. Director: Victor Fleming. Judy Garland, Frank Morgan, Bert Lahr, Jack Haley, Ray Bolger, Billie Burke, Margaret Hamilton. Sure, you have seen this classic plenty of times, but did you ever notice that Dorothy Gale sings that the Wicked Witch was out to "thumb a hitch" in the song "Ding Dong The Witch is Dead"?

INDEX

Adams, Douglas — 79+
adventure, sense of — 28
advertising — 21+
alcohol — 58,94
Alger, Horatio — 25
alienation — 17
Anderson, Raymond L. — 114
animals — 59
attitude — 108+
bag, sleeping — 47,95+
bags, plastic — 47,54
Banner, David — 26
Berg, Rick — 59,76
book(s) — 29,58
Boone, Daniel — 13
boots — 47,50
bum, noun — 8
Burnvand, Jan Harold — 25,28
Buryn, Ed — 9,88,108
camera — 45,47
camping gear — 47,95
canteen — 47,57
cartoons — 23
Chesterton, G. K. — 104
clean, staying — 46
clothes — 47
comb — 47
compass — 47
Coopersmith, Paul — 45
condoms — 51
confidence — 70,108+
cooking gear — 47
corkscrew — 47
crime — 13
crime reports — 13
Crockett, Davy — 13,25
Depression, The — 11,25
disclaimer — 2,69
DiMaggio, Paul — 7,91
drivers — 84+
drugs — 58
economy — 11,15
Eighties, the — 17

eye contact — 70,77
female(s), hitchhiking — 60+
Finn, Huck — 13,26
first aid kit — 47,56
Flanders, Jack — 52
flashlight — 47
food — 55
footwear — 52
freedom — 20,28
Fugitive, The — 26
Gale, Dorothy — 24,133
Garrison, Daniel — 16
gear, camping — 47
gear, cooking — 47
gear not to take — 58
glasses — 47
Gould, Elise — 64
Graham, Janet — 42,62
Grimm, Tom — 36
growth, personal — 37
Guinness Book of
  World Records — 7,114
Guthrie, Woody — 10
Hardyman, Hugh — 11,33,34,
  45,55,97,
Harry, Deborah — 62
hassles, hitchhiking — 91+
hat — 47,96
Heaven, Highway to — 27
helpful, desire to be — 18,87
hitchhike, reasons not to — 37,91+
hitchhike, reasons to — 33+
hitchhike, verb — 8
hitchhiker, image — 21+,48
hitchhiker, noun — 8
hitchhiker, sex of — 42,60+
hitchhiker stereotypes — 21
hitchhiker, vanishing — 28
hitchhikers, female — 60+
hitchhikers, gear — 45,95+
hitchhikers, identification — 48,55
hitchhiking in advertisements — 21+
hitchhiking, attitude — 108+

hitchhiking, cartoons 23
hitchhiking, confidence 70,108+
hitchhiking, hassles 91+
hitchhiking, in towns or cities 74
hitchhiking, laws 15
hitchhiking, legality of 15
hitchhiking, literature 29+
hitchhiking, location 71
hitchhiking, media images 21+,48
hitchhiking, memories 104+,115
hitchhiking, at night 74
hitchhiking, planning 39+,45,96
hitchhiking signs 77+
hitchhiking, songs about 24
hitchhiking, stances 69
hitchhiking, studies of 14,61,111
hitchhiking, time of day 41
hitchhiking, why you
  were picked up 85+
hitchhiking, with others 42+
hitchhiking, worries 91+
hobo, noun 8
Hulk, The Incredible 26
identification 48,55
karma 56,108
Kerouac, Jack 13,76
Kimble, Dr. Richard 26
Kipling, Rudyard 77
Knies, Donald 33,51
knife(s) 47,56
Least Heat Moon,
  William 37,54,59,69,84
librarian(s) 40
library(s) 40,81
location, hitchhiking 71
London, Jack 10,34,91
maps 41,48,53
matches 48,52
memories 104+,115
Michener, James 11,77
migrant workers 17
military 13
Mines, Stephanie 9,88,108
Mishima, Yukio 109
money 48,53
Moriarty, Dean 13,76

neatness 46,49,57
Newman, Steven M. 39
night, hitchhiking at 74
Opus, P. 23
Oz, Wizard of 133
pack(s) 45,47,57
Packard, Reynolds 104
paper 48,104
paper, toilet 47
pen(s) 47
pencil(s) 47
people, meeting 33,35,84+
pet(s) 59
plastic, bags 47,57
police 92+
poncho 47,49
Post, Emily 12
Pratt, Daniel 9
rest stops 57,75
restaurants 56
rides, choosing 84+
risk taking 16
roads, four-lane 40
roads, two-lane 40
Robbins, Tom 19,60,101
Roosevelt, Mrs. Franklin D. 12
safety 71
Sawyer, Tom 12
servicemen 13
Seventies, the 12
sex 60+,101
Shmoo 19
shoulder, road 15
signs 52,78+
Sixties, the 12
sleeping, bag 47,51,97
slogans, sign 80
smile 77
Smith, Devon 7
sneakers 47
soap 47
songs 24
Spence, Steve 94,109,115
stances, thumbing 69+
Steele, Sonny 29
Steinbeck, John 10

Stevenson, Robert Louis	71	University of Colorado	14,111
stove, butane	47	vagabonding	9
suitcase(s)	45	wanderlust	9+
sunglasses	48	War, Vietnam	14
television	21+	War, World II	12
tent	47	watch	47
Thoreau, Henry David	71	water	55
Thumb, Golden	7	weapon(s)	58,59,61
thumbing stances	69+	weather	40,96
toilet articles	47	*Wizard of Oz*	133
toothbrush	47	women hitchhikers	60+,101+
towel	47,79+	W.P.A.	40
tramp, noun	8	Zeidman, Samuel D.	8,38
Tully, Jim	10		

ORDER FORM

Lies Told Press, Ltd.
P.O. Box 2164,
South Hackensack, New Jersey 07606-2164

Please send me _____ copies of Hitchhiking in America; Using the Golden Thumb! $9.00 each.

I enclose $_____

NAME _____

ADDRESS _____

TOWN _____

STATE _____ ZIP CODE _____

For my own curiosity, how did you happen to hear of this book?

_____
_____
_____
_____
_____
_____